Tadao ANDO

Tadao Ando

Tadao Ando

teNeues

Editor in chief:
Paco Asensio

Editor and original texts:
Aurora Cuito

English translation:
William Bain

German translation:
Martin Fischer

French translation:
Agencia Lingo Sense

Italian translation:
Grazia Sufritti

Art direction:
Mireia Casanovas Soley

Graphic Design / Layout:
Emma Termes Parera and Soti Mas-Bagà

Published worldwide by teNeues Publishing Group
(except Spain, Portugal and South-America):

teNeues Book Division
Kaistraße 18, 40221 Düsseldorf, Germany
Tel.: 0049-(0)211-994597-0
Fax: 0049-(0)211-994597-40

teNeues Publishing Company
16 West 22nd Street, New York, N.Y., 10010, USA
Tel.: 001-212-627-9090
Fax: 001-212-627-9511

teNeues Publishing UK Ltd.
P.O. Box 402
West Byfleet
KT14 7ZF
Tel.: 0044-1932-403509
Fax: 0044-1932-403514

teNeues France S.A.R.L.
140, rue de la Croix Nivert
75015 Paris, France
Tel.: 0033-1-5576-6205
Fax: 0033-1-5576-6419

www.teneues.com

Editorial project:

Via Laietana, 32 4° Of. 92
08003 Barcelona, Spain
Tel.: 0034 932 688 088
Fax: 0034 932 687 073
e-mail: loft@loftpublications.com
www.loftpublications.com

Printed by:
Anman Gràfiques del Vallès. Spain
June 2003

Bibliographic information published by Die Deutsche Bibliothek
Die Deutsche Bibliothek lists this publication in the Deutsche Nationalbibliografie; detailed bibliographic data is available in the Internet at http://dnb.ddb.de.

ISBN: 3-8238-4538-1

We would like to show sincere gratefulness to the office of Tadao Ando, specially to Hiroshi Araki and Antoine Müller Moriya for their useful collaboration.

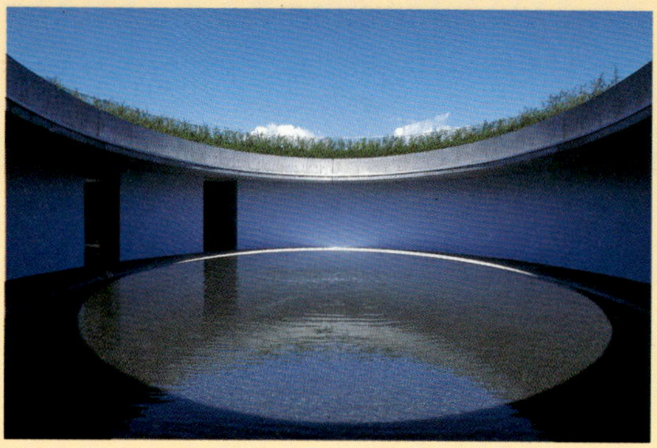

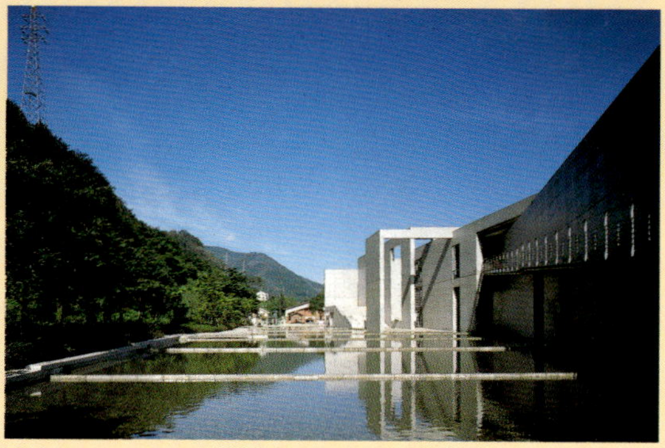

Tadao Ando, a disciplined autodidact, got an education that would seem to be somewhere between the Japanese tradition and the rationalist influences he has been able to observe on his trips to Europe and the United States. Thus has he learned from the great masters of the twentieth century such as Le Corbusier, Alvar Aalto, and Mies van der Rohe. But his own scrupulousness for details, seen in the finishes he gives his buildings, have made Ando a refined creator, an irreproachable builder.

While his career includes many different typologies, from single-family dwellings like the Row House in Sumiyoshi (Osaka, 1975) to churches such as the Church on the Water (Hokkaido, 1985), or pavilions such as the one he built for the Seville Expo (1992), one also finds outstanding museum projects in this Japanese architect's work. Given his capacity for creating spaces where the relationship between object and observer is optimal, it is in no way strange that he is the author of many cultural complexes in his native country as well as in other parts of the world, notably, the United States and France.

Tadao Ando's ability and expertise reside above all in the generation of exhibition spaces where, in spite of the outside perception, we are invited into the physical and emotional intimacy necessary to admire, understand, and even to interact with the objects displayed.

Tadao Ando hat sich im intensiven Selbststudium sowohl mit der japanischen Tradition als auch mit der rationalistischen Formensprache vertraut gemacht, die er auf seinen Reisen nach Europa und in die Vereinigten Staaten kennenlernte. Er orientierte sich an den großen Meistern des 20. Jahrhunderts wie Le Corbusier, Alvar Aalto und Mies van der Rohe. Ein gewissenhafter Blick für Details und durchdachte Lösungen in der Ausführung lassen ihn zu einem raffinierten Schöpfer, einem hervorragenden Baumeister werden.

Während seiner Architektentätigkeit hat er zwar schon viele unterschiedliche Bauaufgaben gelöst – er schuf Einfamilienhäuser wie das Row House in Sumiyoshi (Osaka, 1975), Kirchen wie die Kapelle über dem Wasser (Hokkaido, 1985) oder den Pavillon auf der Weltausstellung von Sevilla (1992) –, doch unter den zahlreichen Werken des japanischen Meisters stechen besonders seine Entwürfe für Museen hervor. Aufgrund seiner Fähigkeit, Räume mit einer optimalen Beziehung zwischen Objekt und Betrachter zu ersinnen, kann es nicht verwundern, dass er unzählige Aufträge für kulturelle Einrichtungen in seinem Heimatland, aber auch aus dem Ausland erhielt, etwa aus Frankreich oder den USA.

Die Geschicklichkeit und das Fachwissen Tadao Andos treten besonders deutlich zu Tage, wenn es darum geht, Räume der Besinnung zu schaffen, in denen der Besucher trotz der Wahrnehmung der Außenwelt die erforderliche körperliche und seelische Intimität genießt, um die ausgestellten Gegenstände zu bewundern, zu begreifen und sogar mit ihnen in Verbindung zu treten.

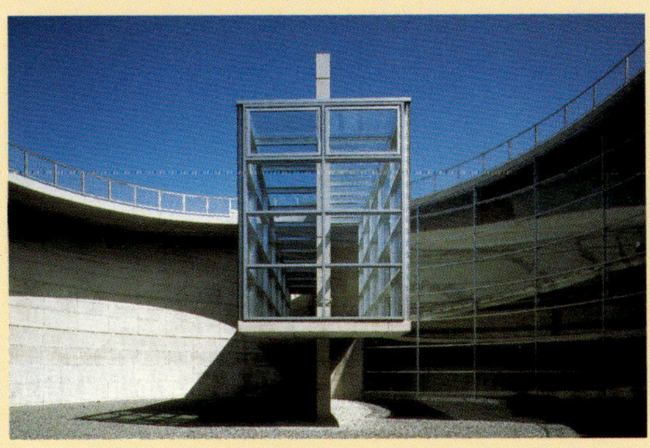

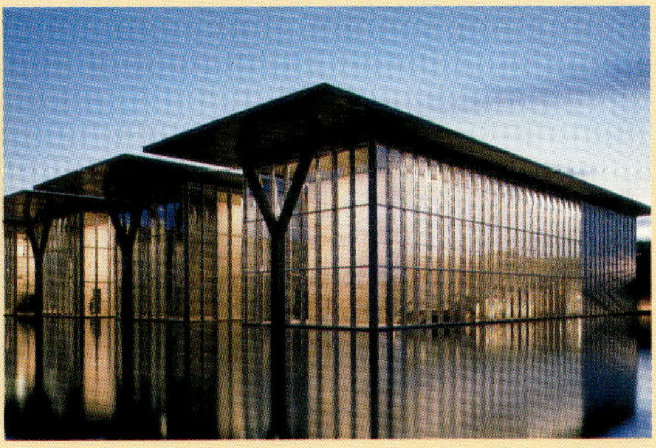

Tadao Ando, autodidacte discipliné, bénéficie d'une formation à cheval entre la tradition nippone et l'influence du langage rationaliste, observé lors de ses voyages en Europe et aux États-Unis. Il a appris des grands maîtres du XXème siècle comme Le Corbusier, Alvar Aalto et Mies van der Rohe. En outre, son souci pour les détails et la sophistication qu'il confère aux finitions de ses constructions en font un créateur raffiné, un bâtisseur sans faille.

Bien que la trajectoire du prolifique architecte japonais comprenne de multiples typologies, des projets résidentiels, tels que la Row House à Sumiyoshi (Osaka, 1975), aux églises comme la chapelle sur l'eau (Hokkaido, 1985) en passant par le pavillon de l'Exposition universelle de Séville (1992), l'on peut cependant mettre en exergue les projets muséographiques. De par sa capacité à créer des espaces où la relation entre l'objet et l'observateur atteint un optimum, il n'est pas étonnant qu'il ait projeté autant de complexes culturels dans son pays natal, comme ailleurs dans le monde, ainsi aux États-Unis ou en France.

La maestria et l'expertise de Tadao Ando résident surtout dans la création d'une ambiance de recueillement où, en dépit d'un extérieur perçu, le spectateur bénéficie de l'intimité physique et émotionnelle nécessaires pour admirer, comprendre, voire interagir avec les objets exposés.

Tadao Ando, disciplinato autodidatta, riceve un'educazione a cavallo tra la tradizione nipponica e le influenze del linguaggio razionalista, quest'ultimo esplorato durante i suoi viaggi in Europa e negli Stati Uniti ed appreso da grandi maestri del XX° secolo, come Le Corbusier, Alvar Aalto e Mies van der Rohe. La sua scrupolosità per i dettagli, evidente nelle sofisticate finiture di cui dota gli edifici, lo trasformano in un raffinato creatore ed un costruttore impeccabile.

Anche se la sua carriera abbraccia molteplici tipologie – che vanno dagli alloggi unifamiliari come la Row House a Sumiyoshi (Osaka, 1975) alle chiese, come la cappella sull'acqua (Hokkaido, 1985), o ai padiglioni, come quello per l'Esposizione Universale di Siviglia (1992) – nell'attività dell'architetto giapponese emergono soprattutto i progetti mu-seali. Data la sua capacità di creare spazi dove la relazione tra oggetto ed osservatore è ottima, non deve sorprendere che abbia progettato numerosi complessi culturali non solo nel suo paese natale, ma anche in altri luoghi del mondo, come Stati Uniti o Francia.

L'abilità e la bravura di Tadao Ando risiedono soprattutto nel realizzare ambienti espositivi dove, nonostante la percezione esterna, lo spettatore gode dell'intimità fisica ed emozionale necessaria per ammirare, comprendere e, perfino, interagire con gli oggetti esposti.

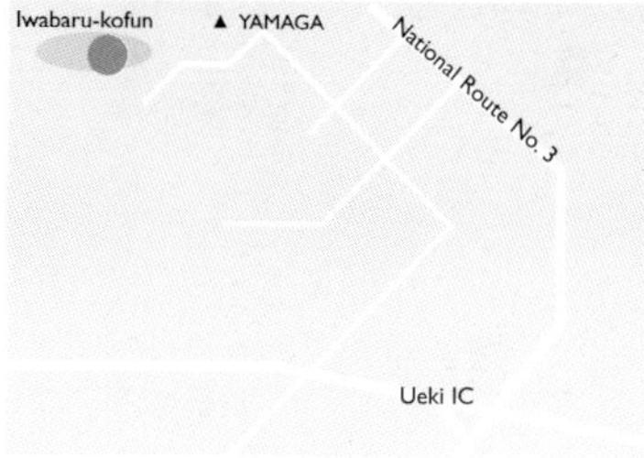

Forest of Tombs Museum

Location: Kamoto, Kumamoto, Japan
Date of construction: 1990–1992
Photographer: Hiroshi Ueda

The region of Kyushu is steeped in ancestral Japanese history. In this mythical zone, in the northern part of the prefecture of Kumamoto, lies the tombs' historical museum of Kamoto. The nearby mortuary complex comprises the Futago-zuka keyhole shaped tumulos, surrounded by eight smaller burial mounds. Given its proportions, the slight incline of the hillsides and the elegance of its contours, Futago-zuka stands out as one of the most beautiful and important deposits in Japan. Conscious of the beauty and the significance of the place, Ando decided to subtly distance himself and not do any work with the tombs. He situated the museum some 250 meters from the tombs. The parking area, still farther away, lies below the natural plateau on which the complex was raised. This whole arrangement allows the visitor to come to the museum after having passed through a lush woodland. One is then in view of the sepulchers but without having reached the architect's contributions. The project's conception aims at transcending the mere spatial relationship between tombs and architectural volume: the museum sweeps up in evocation of the spirit of ancestral structures, a contemporary burial mound.

In der Region Kyushu ist die japanische Frühgeschichte allgegenwärtig. In diesem geschichtsträchtigen Gebiet, im Norden der Präfektur Kumamoto, befindet sich das Grabstättenmuseum Kamoto. Das nahe gelegene Gräberfeld umfasst den schllüssellochförmige Tumulus Futago-zuka, umgeben von acht kleinere Grabhügel. Mit seiner eleganten Proportionen und den sanft abfallenden Hängen gilt Futago-zuka als einer der schönsten und bedeutendsten frühgeschichtlichen Bodenfunde Japans. Ando war sich der Schönheit und der Bedeutung des Ortes bewusst und beschloss daher, sein Projekt etwas abseits der Grabhügel zu verwirklichen, ohne im Denkmalbereich Veränderungen vorzunehmen. Das Museum liegt etwa 250 Meter von den Gräbern entfernt, der Parkplatz ist noch abgelegener, unterhalb der Anhöhe, auf der sich die Anlage befindet. So erreichen die Besucher das Museum, nachdem sie einen dichten Wald durchquert haben, und haben freien Blick auf die Grabhügel, noch bevor sie das eigentliche Museumsgebäude sehen. Der Entwurf sollte über eine schlichte räumliche Beziehung zwischen den Gräbern und den Gebäuden hinausgehen. Deshalb wurde das Museum im Anklang an den Geist der frühgeschichtlichen Zeugnisse errichtet, so als ob es sich um einen Tumulus aus heutiger Zeit handelte.

La région de Kyushu est baignée d'histoire ancestrale japonaise. Dans cette contrée mythique, le nord de la préfecture de Kumamoto abrite le musée funéraire de Kamoto. Le complexe funéraire tout proche comporte le tumulus Futago-zuka en forme de trou de serrure, entouré de huit plus petits monticules sépulcraux. De par ses proportions, la pente mesurée de ses versants et l'élégance de ses formes, le Futago-zuka se présente comme l'un des sites les plus beaux et importants du Japon. Conscient de cette beauté et de la signification du lieu, Ando décida de s'éloigner subtilement et de ne pas intervenir sur les tombes. Il situa le musée à quelques 250 mètres du site et éloigna encore davantage le parking, en contrebas du petit plateau naturel où se trouve l'ensemble. De cette manière, le visiteur arrive au musée après être passé par un bois luxuriant et peut profiter des vues sur les sépultures, sans intervention additionnelle de l'architecte. La conception du projet avait pour fin de transcender la simple relation spatiale entre les tombes et le volume construit. Le musée a donc été créé en une évocation de l'esprit des constructions ancestrales, comme un tumulus contemporain.

La regione di Kyushu è impregnata di antica storia giapponese. In questa mitica zona, al nord della prefettura di Kumamoto, si trova il museo funerario di Kamoto. Il vicino complesso mortuario Futago-zuka consiste in un tumulo a forma di foro di serratura, circondato da otto piú piccoli monticelli sepolcrali. Per le sue proporzioni, la misurata inclinazione dei pendii e l'eleganza delle sue forme, il Futago-zuka si distingue come una delle zone archeologiche più importanti e belle del Giappone. Cosciente della bellezza e del significato del luogo, Ando ha deciso di prenderne le distanze e non intervenire sulle tombe. Ha situato il museo a circa 250 metri dalla zona archeologica, ed ha collocato il parcheggio ancora più lontano, sotto il piccolo pianoro naturale dove sorge il complesso. In questo modo il visitatore arriva al museo dopo aver attraversato un bosco rigoglioso e può contemplare la vista dei sepolcri prima di aver raggiunto gli altri interventi dell'architetto. La concezione del progetto ha voluto trascendere la mera relazione spaziale tra le tombe ed il volume architettonico, ed il museo è stato eretto secondo un'evocazione dello spirito delle costruzioni ancestrali, come se si trattasse di un sepolcro contemporaneo.

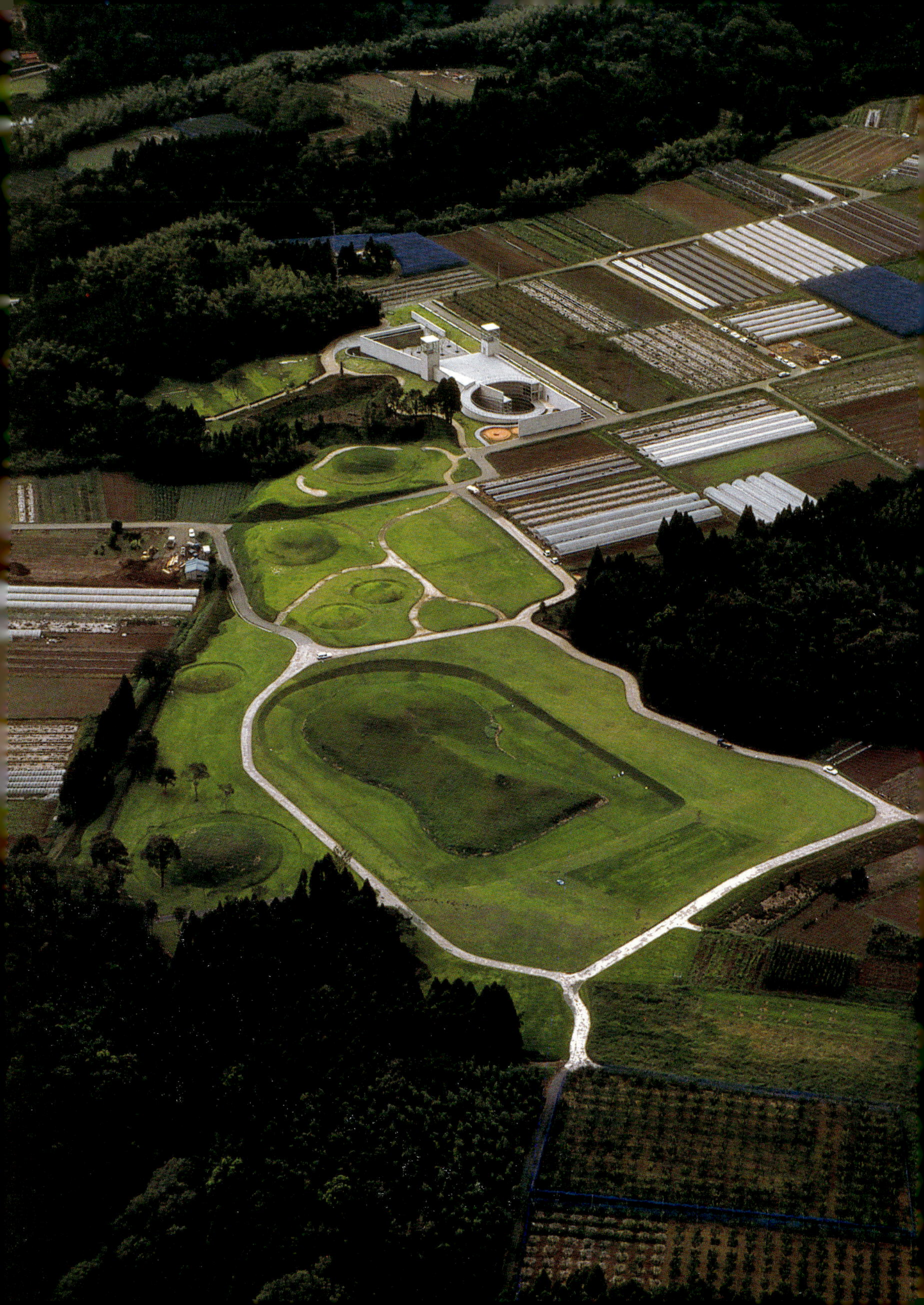

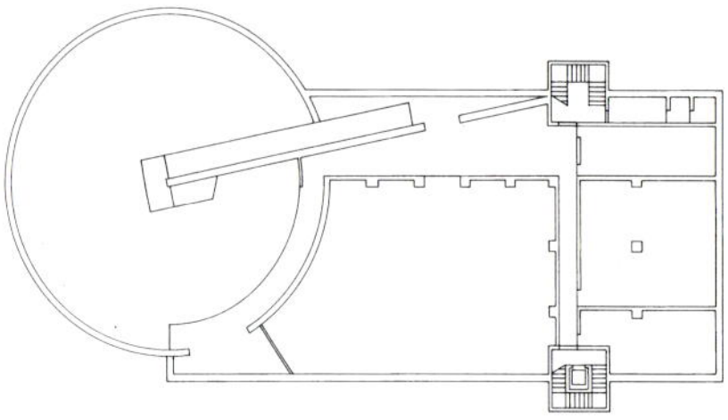

Basement Souterrain
Sous-sol **Piano interrato**

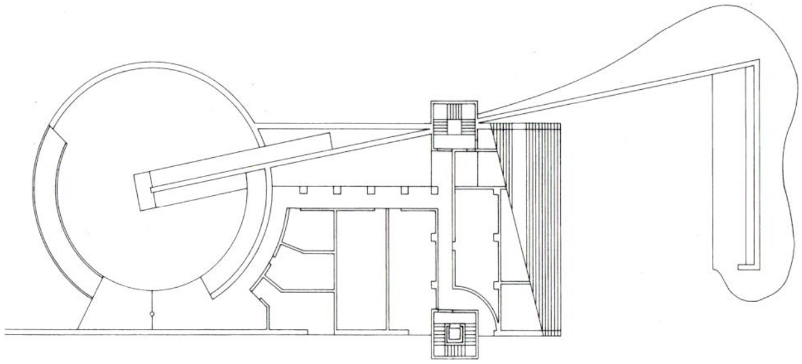

Ground floor Erdgeschoss
Rez-de-chaussée **Piano terra**

0 7 14

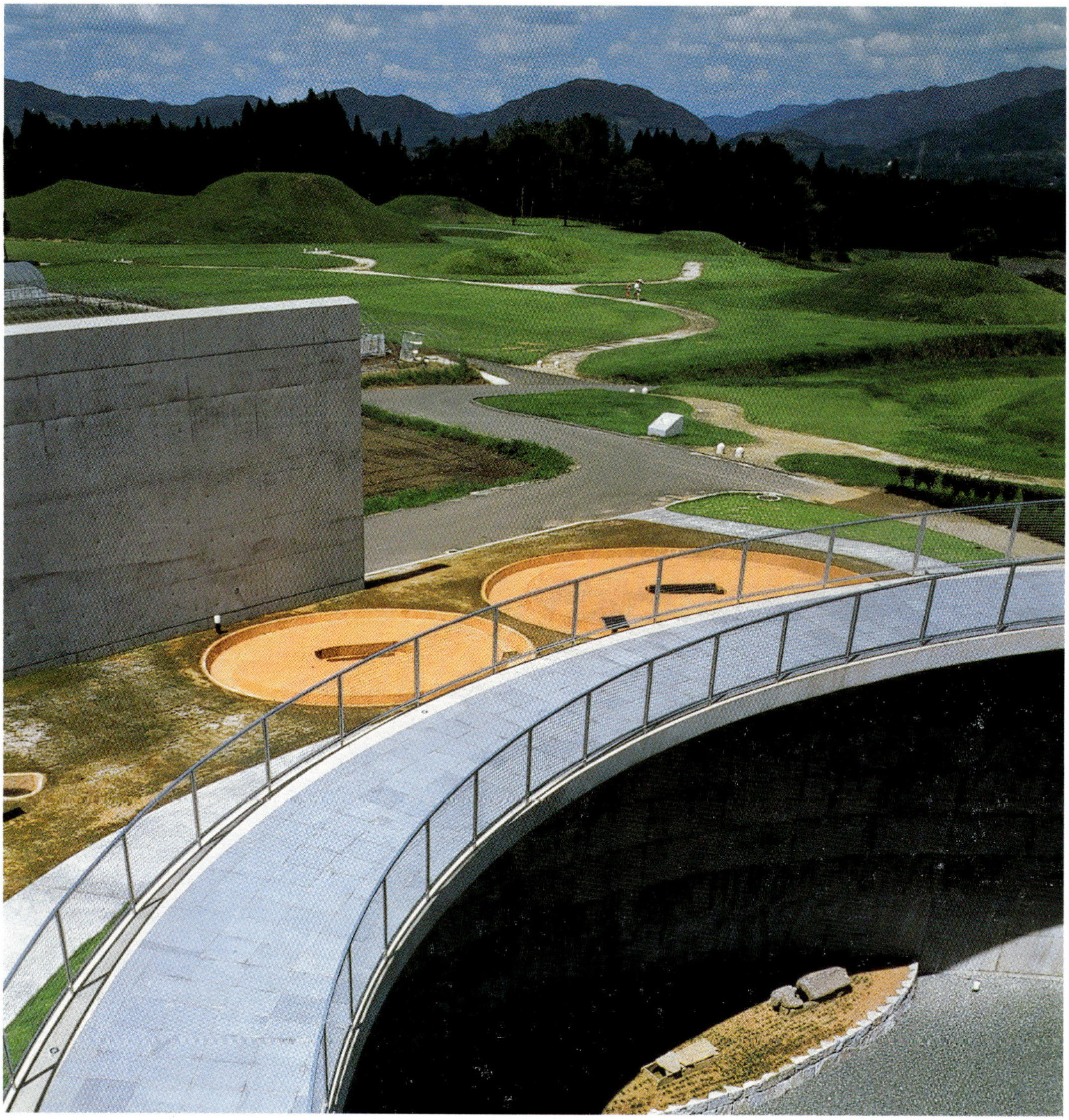

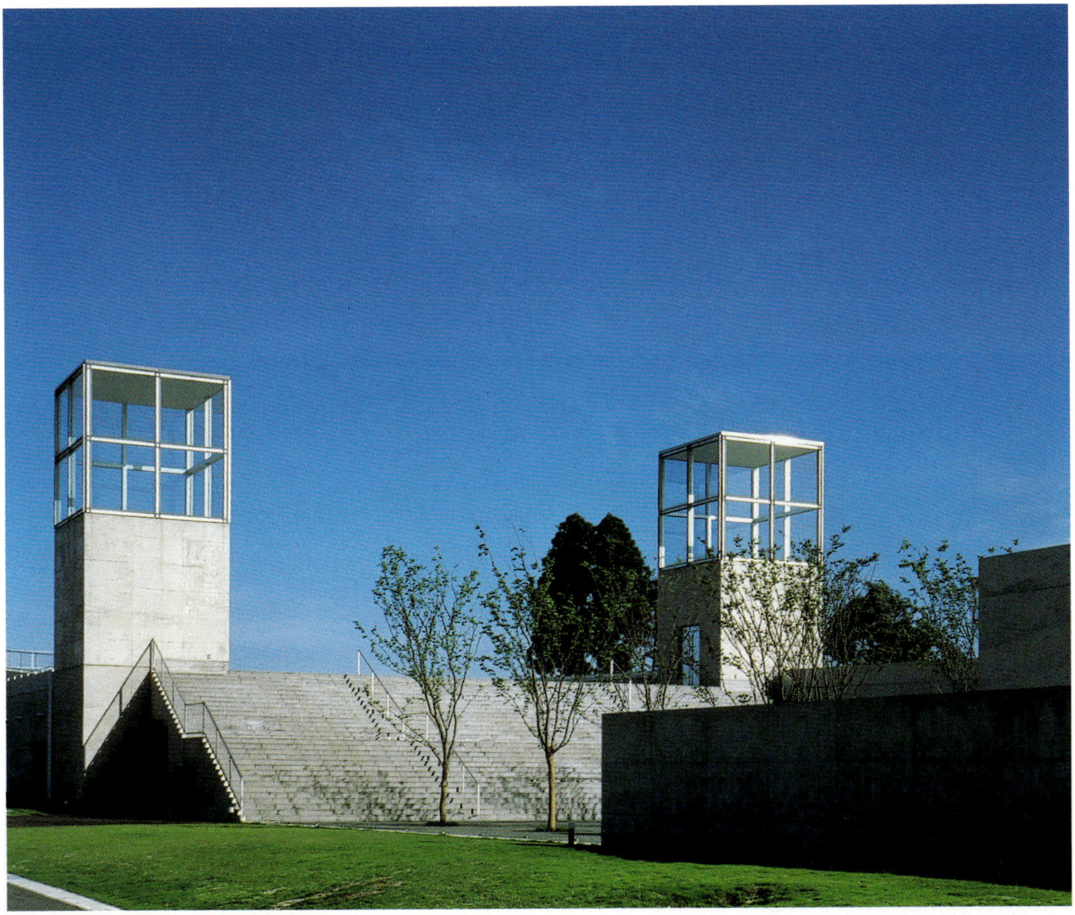

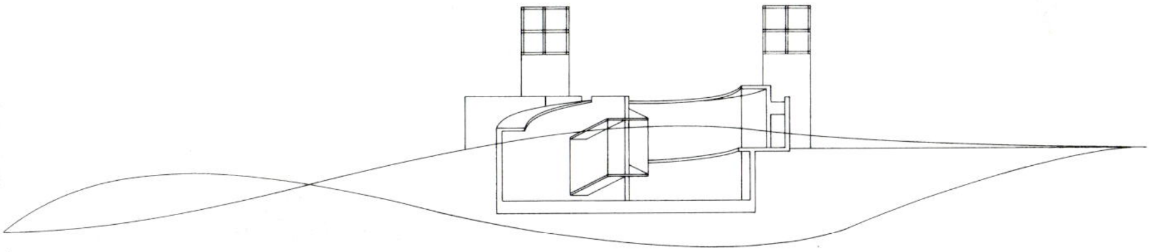

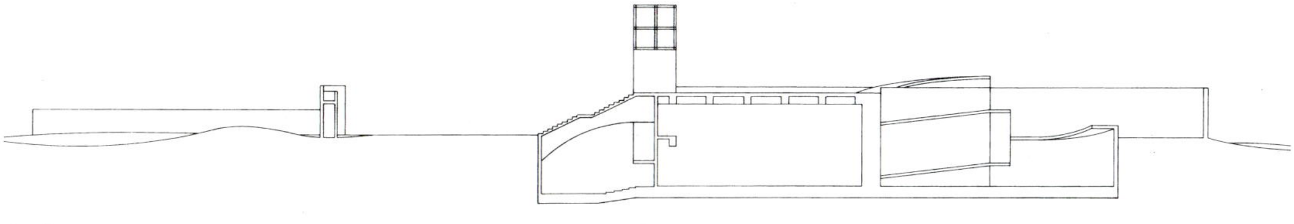

Sections
Schnitte
Sections
Sezioni

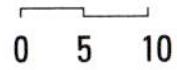

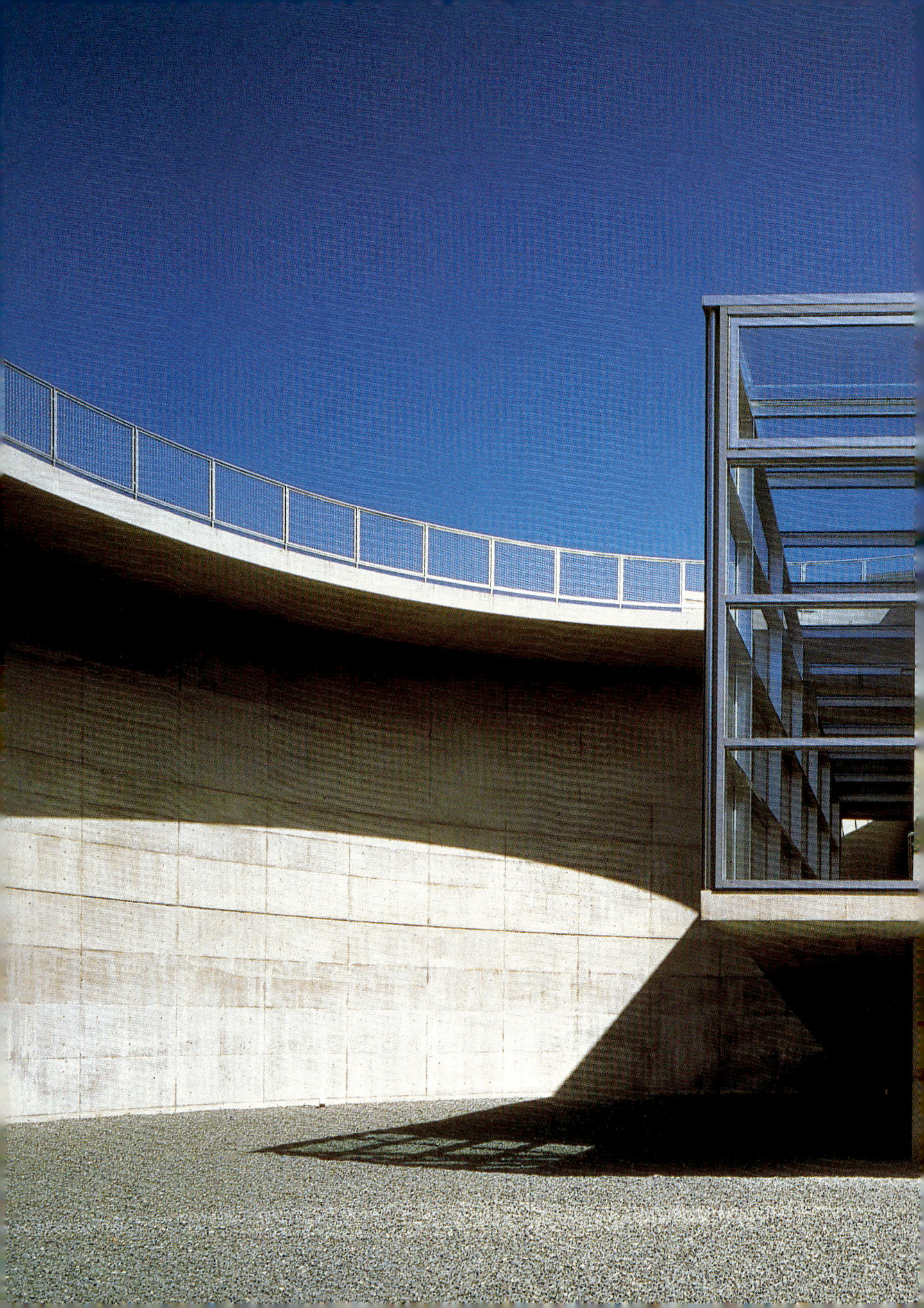

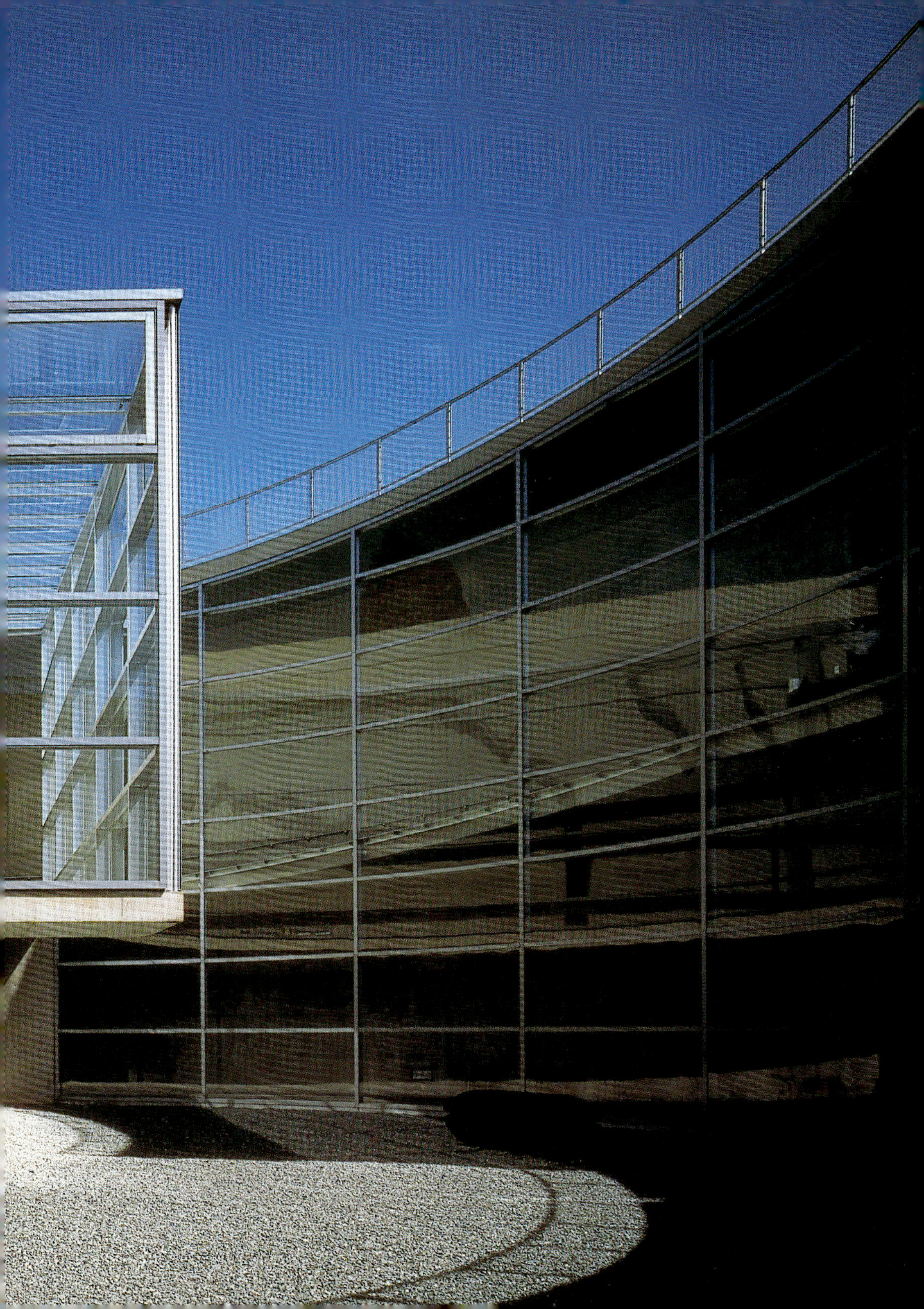

Naoshima Contemporary Art Museum & Annex

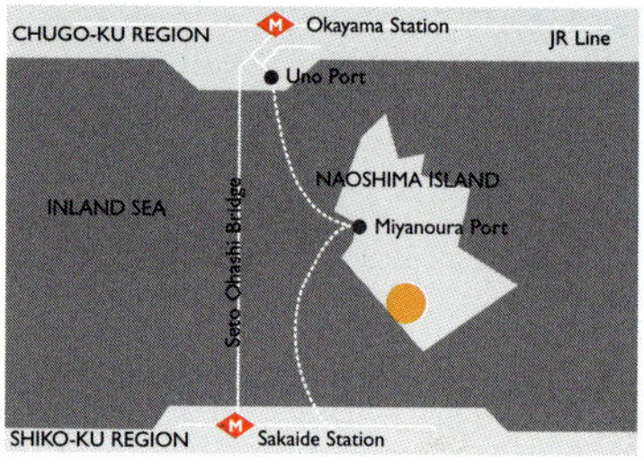

Location: Naoshima, Kagawa, Japan
Date of construction: 1990–1992
Photographers: Mitsuo Matsuoka, Hiroshi Ueda, Shigeo Ogawa, Tadao Ando

The museum is on a hillside in a cape to the southeast of the Naoshima Island. It overlooks a quiet beach located just at the base of the slope. Due to the layout of the project visitors access directly from the wharf, which leads to a stepped plaza and which serves as a kind of stage setting for open-air activities, on the roof of a detached gallery. The subtlety with which Ando has arranged more than half of the total volume of the museum as subterranean spaces makes it possible to contemplate the magnificent national park surrounding the area uninterruptedly. On mounting the stairs of the plaza, the stone walls giving shape to the museum itself are perceived. After passing the entrance hall, one comes to an enormous sunken gallery, fully fifty meters long and two stories high. The greater part of the complex, including the hotel, the exhibition galleries, the terraces and the later added annex building on the hilltop give onto the ocean and introduce great tranquility into the interior spaces. From these spaces one finds oneself looking out onto the maritime sunsets and the coming and going of the ships. The whole piece, like the sculptures in its gardens, is a magistral use of nature to create a new landscape.

Le musée se trouve sur la pente d'un cap, au sud est de l'île de Naoshima et domine une plage tranquille située plus bas. L'implantation du projet est telle que les visiteurs accèdent au museé directement depuis un embarcadère, menant à une place en terrasses tenant lieu de seuil et de scène pour des activités à l'air libre tout en couvrant un pavillon d'exposition. La subtilité avec laquelle Ando a disposé la moitié du volume construit sous terre permet de préserver la continuité du magnifique parc national environnant. En gravissant les escaliers de la place, les murs de pierre formant le musée deviennent progressivement perceptibles. Aprés avoir franchi le hall d'entrée, l'on aboutit à une vaste galerie enterrée, de cinquante mètres de long et sur deux niveaux. La majorité des espaces du complexe, incluant l'hôtel, les galeries d'exposition, les terrasses et l'annexe construite plus tard au sommet de la pente s'ouvre sur la mer et introduit dans les espaces intérieurs la tranquillité offerte par la contemplation des couchers de soleil marins et le va-et-vient des navires. L'œuvre, comme les sculptures en plain air, utilise magistralement la nature pour créer un nouveau paysage.

Das Museum befindet sich am Hang einer Landzunge im Südosten der Insel Naoshima, oberhalb eines ruhigen Strandes. Die Besucher gelangen direkt von einer Schiffsanlegestelle zur Anlage, und zwar zunächst auf einen Platz, der über einem unterirdischen Nebengalerie angelegt wurde, als Eingangsbereich dient und zugleich für Veranstaltungen unter freiem Himmel genutzt werden kann. Durch Andos Kunstgriff, mehr als die Hälfte des Bauvolumens unter die Erdoberfläche zu verlegen, können die Besucher die herrliche Landschaft des umgebenden Nationalparks ungehindert genießen. Wenn man vom Platz kommend die Stufen emporsteigt, erblickt man die Steinmauern des Museums und erreicht dann die Eingangshalle und eine eindrucksvolle, fünfzig Meter lange zweigeschossige Galerie, die in den Hang eingebettet wurde. Die meisten Teile der Anlage – Ausstellungsräume, ein Hotel, Terrassen sowie das später gebaute Nebengebäude auf dem Gipfel – öffnen sich zum Meer hin und geben so den Besuchern die Möglichkeit, sich aus den Innenräumen heraus an der beruhigenden Wirkung zu erfreuen, die von den Sonnenuntergängen über dem Meer und dem Ein- und Auslaufen der Schiffe ausgeht. Der Museumskomplex mit seinen Skulpturengärten nutzt die umgebende Natur meisterlich zur Schaffung einer neuen Landschaft.

Il museo si trova sul pendio di un promontorio, a sud-est dell'isola di Naoshima, e si affaccia su una tranquilla spiaggia situata alla base. La disposizione del progetto è tale che i visitatori accedono al luogo d'esposizione direttamente dal pontile, il quale conduce ad una piazza che funge da ingresso serve come palcoscenico per attività all'aria aperta ed è la copertura d'una galleria sotterranea annessa. La finezza con la quale Ando dispone più della metà del volume totale dell'intervento sottoterra, permette di contemplare il magnifico parco nazionale circostante. Salendo le scalinate della piazza si scorgono i muri di pietra che modellano il museo. Passando per la sala d'ingresso, si giunge ad un'enorme galleria sotterranea, di cinquanta metri di lunghezza e due piani d'altezza. La maggior parte degli spazi del complesso, inclusi l'hotel, le gallerie d'esposizione, le terrazze e l'edificio annesso aggiunto successivamente sulla cima del monte, si aprono verso il mare e fanno penetrare nelle stanze interne la tranquillità che offre la contemplazione dei tramonti marittimi ed il via vai delle barche. L'opera, come le sculture all'aria aperta, rappresenta un eccellente impiego della natura nella creazione di un nuovo paesaggio.

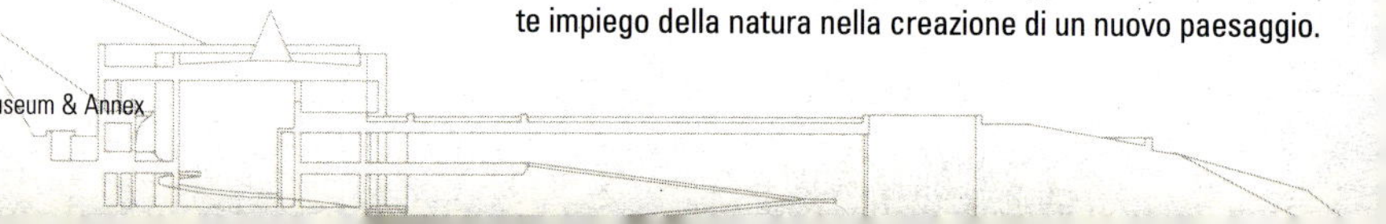

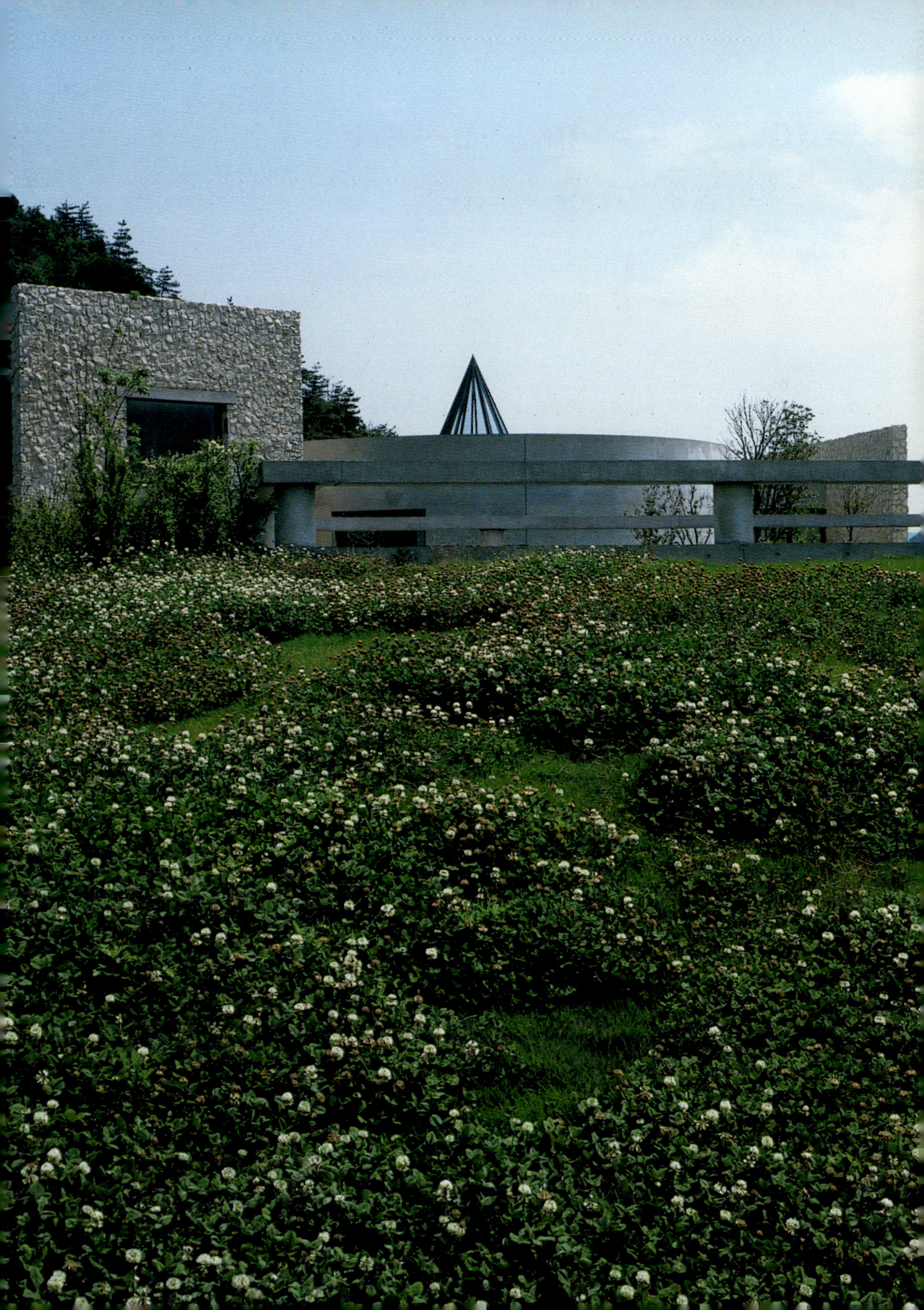

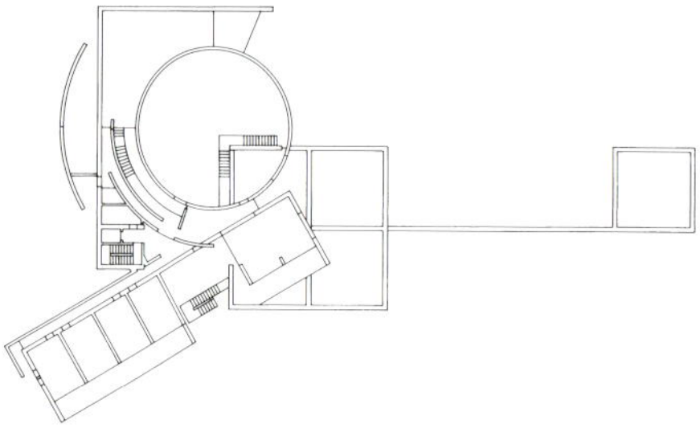

First floor Premier étage

Erstes Obergeschoss **Piano primo**

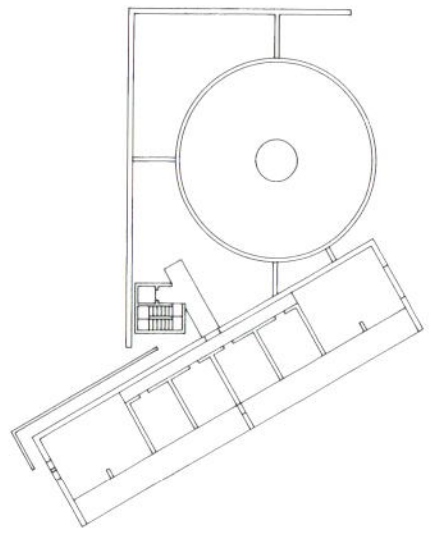

Second floor Deuxième étage

Zweites Obergeschoss **Piano secondo**

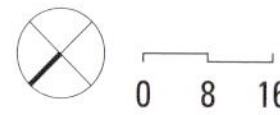

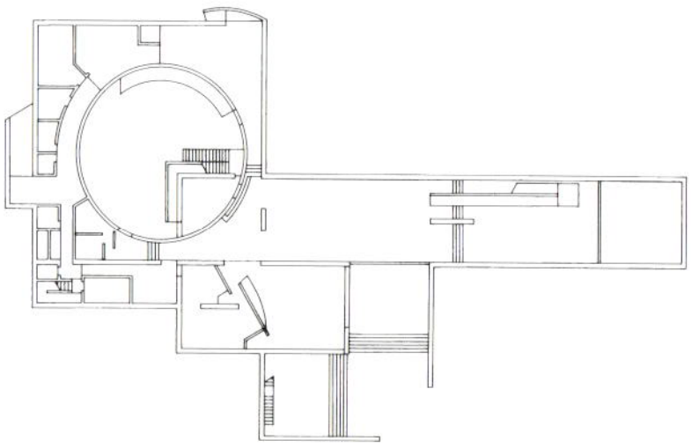

Basement Sous-sol

Souterrain **Piano interrato**

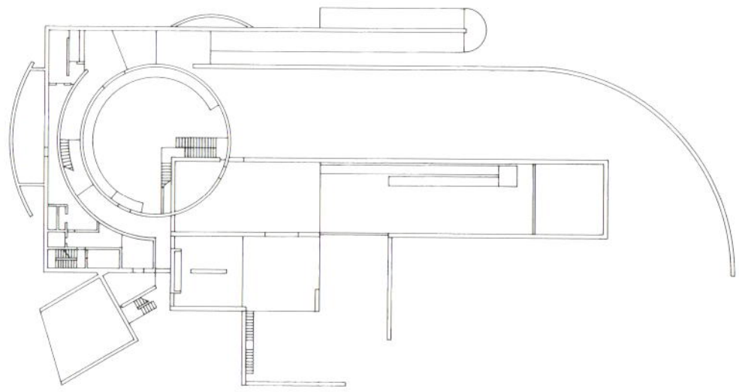

Ground floor Rez-de-chaussée

Erdgeschoss **Piano terra**

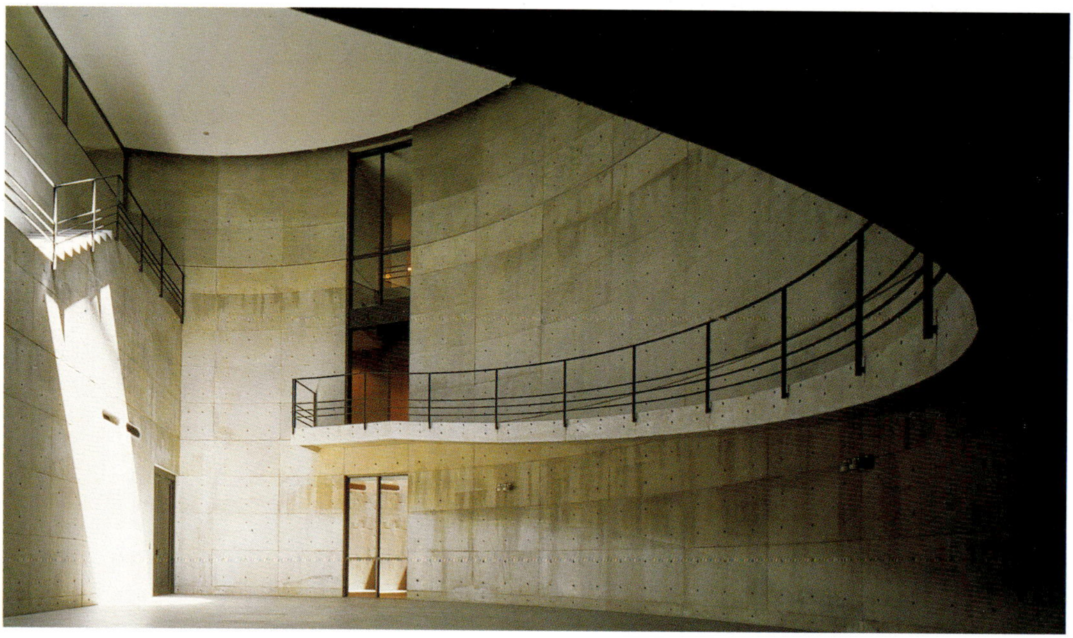

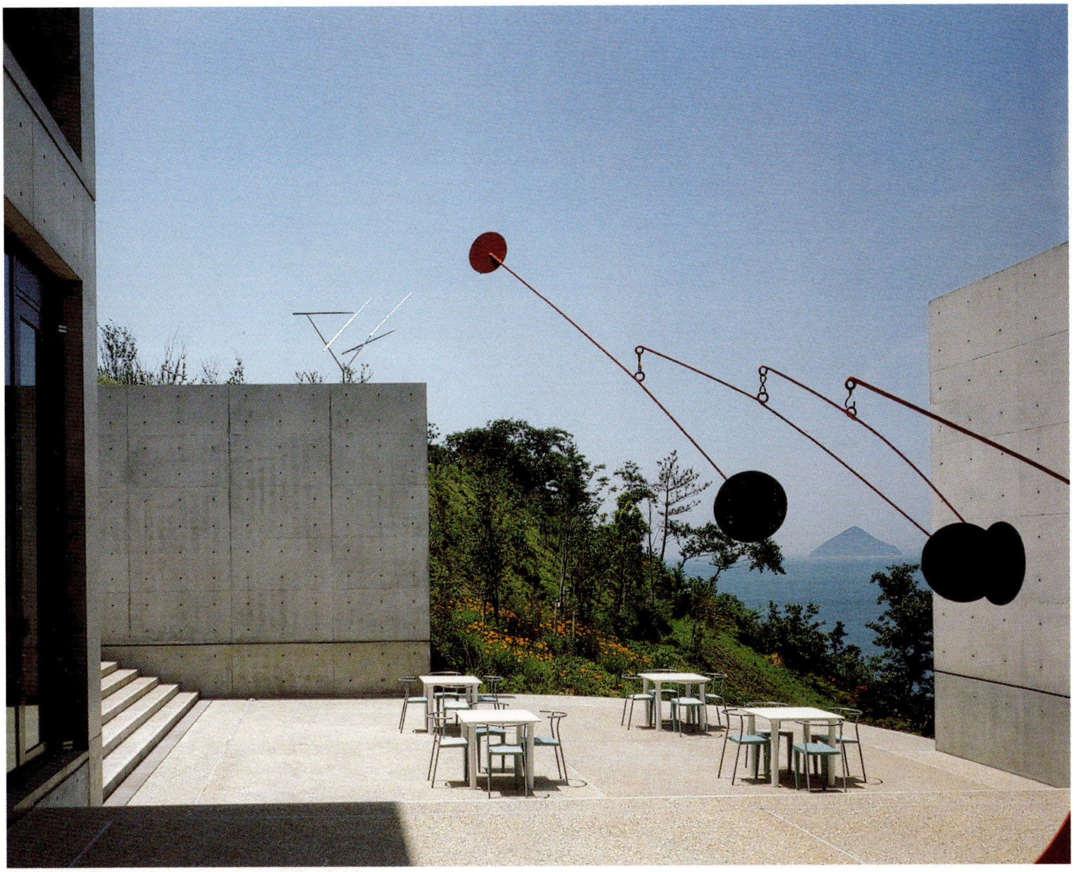

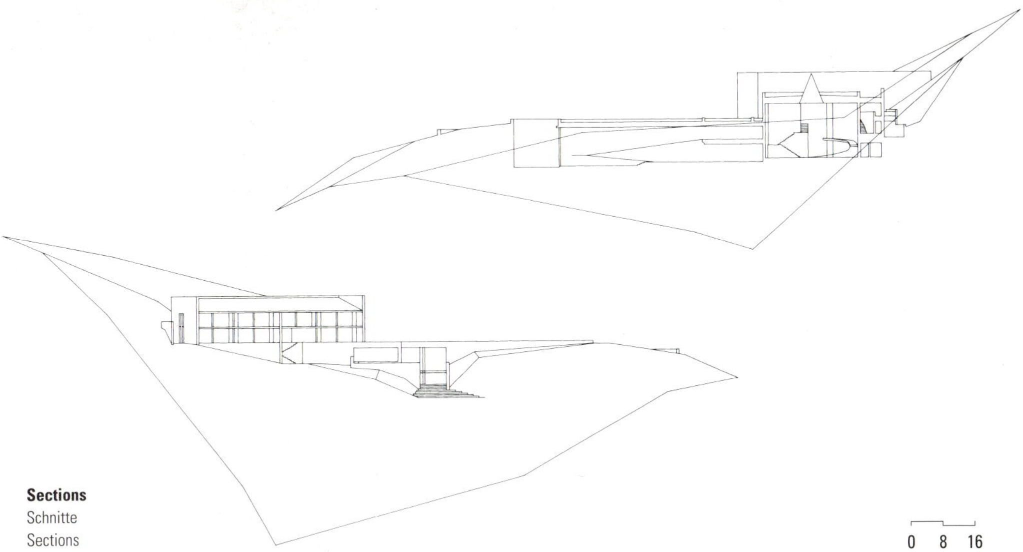

Sections
Schnitte
Sections
Sezioni

0 8 16

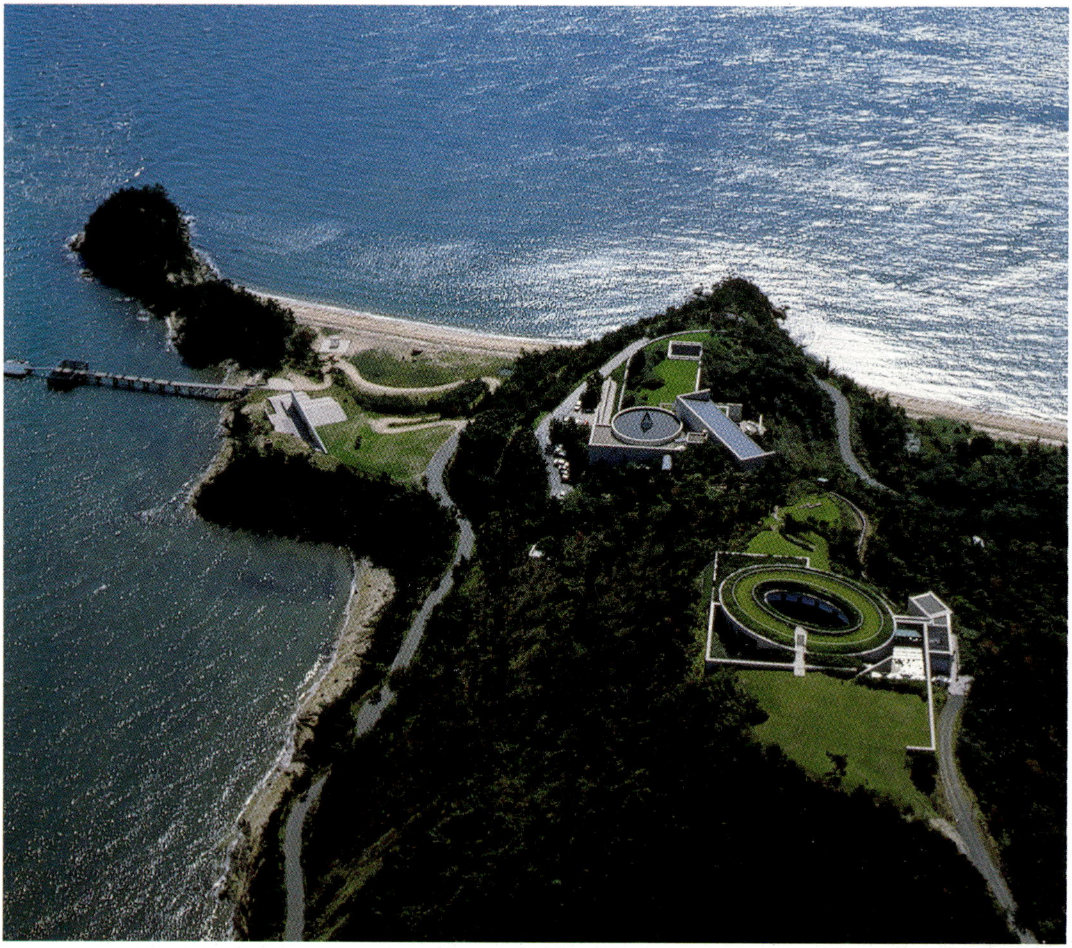

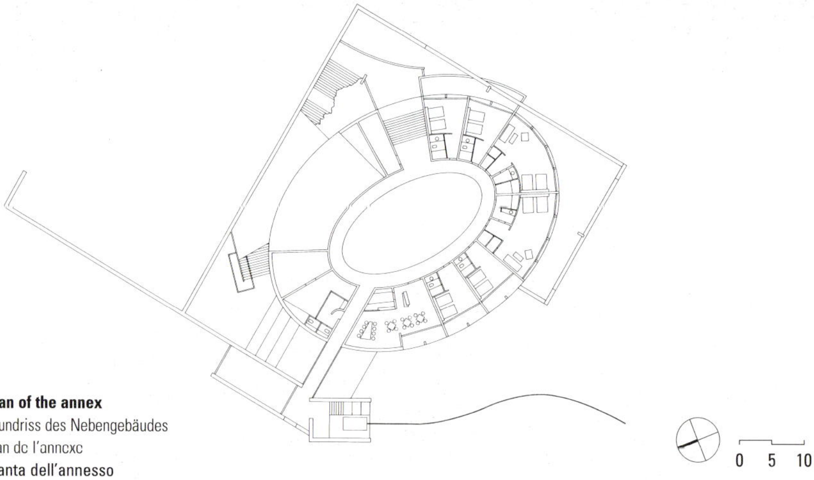

Plan of the annex
Grundriss des Nebengebäudes
Plan de l'annexe
Pianta dell'annesso

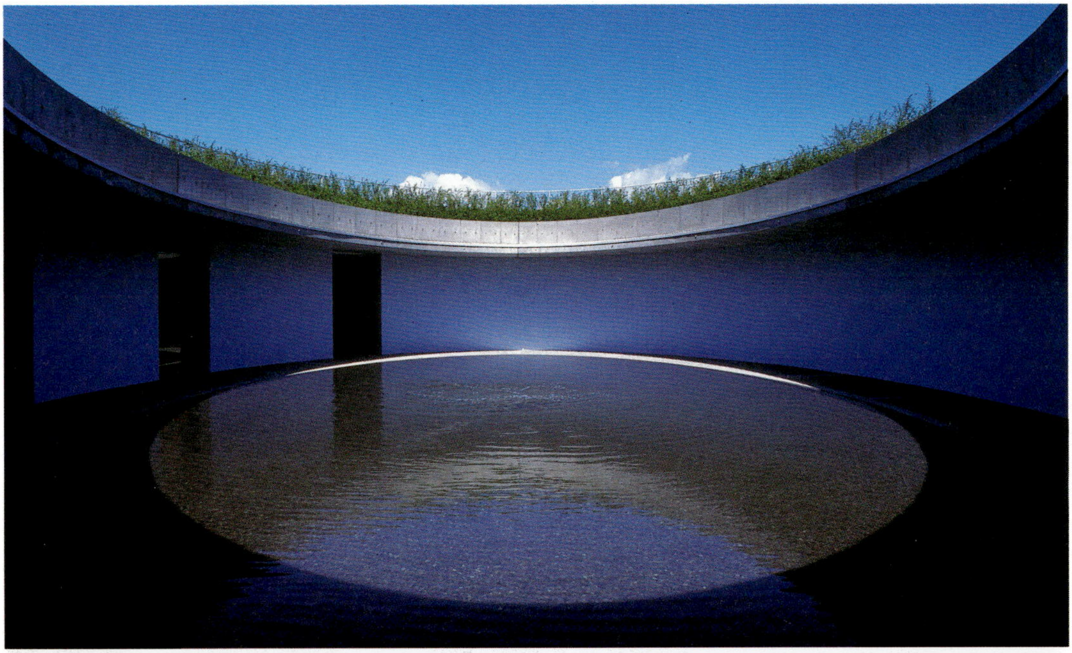

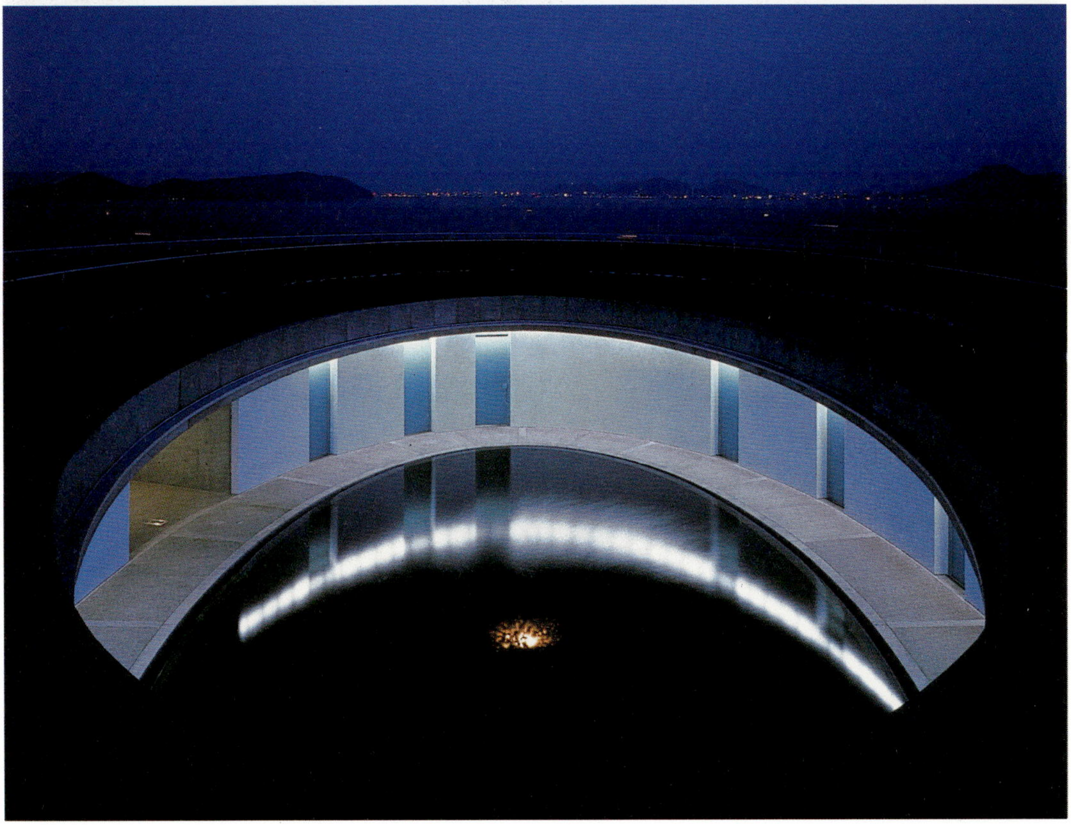

Gallery for Japanese Screens

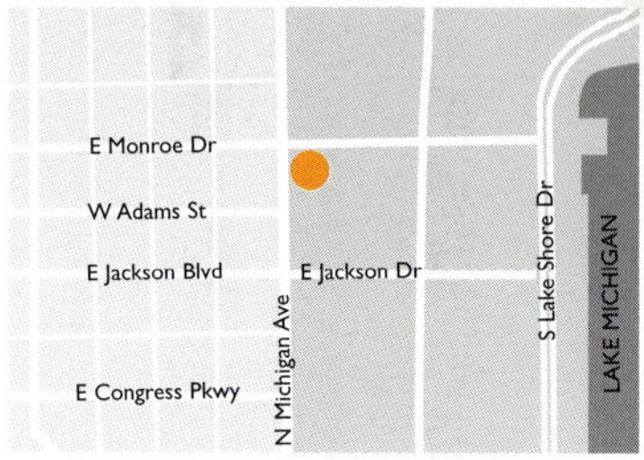

Location: The Art Institute of Chicago, Illinois, USA
Date of construction: 1991–1992
Photographer: Mitsuo Matsuoka

Here, the monumental scale and the quality of the works contained within make the Art Institute of Chicago one of the most important museums in the United States. On the shores of Lake Michigan, the museum is known for its collection of Japanese ukiyoe prints and French Impressionist painting. It also contains an important collection of Asiatic art, at present in process of expansion. The project commissioned to Ando consisted in designing a gallery to exhibit the Japanese ceramics and screens. The space was bisected into two zones, one of which was provided with a network of columns thirty centimeters wide and three meters in height. They serve to mark the depth of this space and generate multiple views that change according to whether the view we receive is foreshortened or not. There is also the aspect of the way the columnar web recreates the spirit of the Japanese room, where fine wooden mounts and the translucence of the panels bring about dynamic spaces. They are spaces rich in plays of light and shadow. What Ando definitely did is to display the screens to their optimal advantage and to involve the spectator in a typically Japanese ontology.

Das Art Institute of Chicago ist dank seiner monumentalen Ausmaße und der Qualität der ausgestellten Werke eines der wichtigsten Museen der Vereinigten Staaten. Es liegt am Michigan-See und ist vor allem wegen seiner Sammlung japanischer Holzschnitte und seiner Gemälde französischer Impressionisten bekannt. Außerdem beherbergt es eine wichtige Sammlung asiatischer Kunst, die momentan noch ausgeweitet wird. Ando erhielt den Auftrag, eine Galerie für Keramik und Paravents aus Japan zu errichten. Er teilte den Raum in zwei Hälften und stellte in einen von ihnen ein Raster aus dreißig Zentimeter starken und drei Meter hohen Pfeilern, die die Tiefe des Raumes betonen und verschiedenartige Ansichten ermöglichen, je nachdem ob man sie von vorne oder in perspektivischer Verkürzung sieht. Der Architekt empfindet auf diese Weise den Geist japanischer Architektur nach, in der die schmalen Holzrahmen und die Transparenz der Paravents dynamische Räume mit reichem Licht- und Schattenspiel schaffen. So gelang es Ando, die Paravents in einer typisch japanischen Atmosphäre angemessen zur Schau zu stellen.

Grâce à son échelle monumentale et à la qualité des œuvres qu'il accueille, l'Art Institute de Chicago est l'un de musées les plus importants des États-Unis. Au bord du lac Michigan, l'institution est connue pour sa collection d'estampes japonaises et de peintures impressionnistes françaises. Il abrite également un ensemble d'œuvres d'art asiatiques, actuellement en cours de constitution. Ando s'est vu chargé de projeter une galerie pour l'exposition de céramiques et de paravents japonais. L'espace a été divisé en deux zones. L'une des deux a été peuplée d'un réseau de colonnes de trente centimètres de côté par trois mètres de haut. Ces piliers ont pour but de marquer la profondeur de l'espace et de générer des points de vue multiples, selon le regard porté de face ou en perspective. Ils recréent aussi l'esprit des intérieurs japonais dont les fins montants de bois et la translucidité des écrans engendrent des espaces dynamiques, riches en jeux d'ombre et de lumière. L'architecte parvient à exposer les panneaux dans des conditions optimales tout en enveloppant l'observateur dans une atmosphère typiquement japonaise.

Grazie alle sue dimensioni monumentali ed alla qualità delle opere che raccoglie, l'Art Institute of Chicago è uno dei musei più importanti degli Stati Uniti. Situato sulle rive del lago Michigan, l'istituzione è famosa per la sua collezione di stampe giapponesi e di pittura impressionista francese. Ospita anche un'importante collezione di arte asiatica, attualmente in espansione. Il progetto di cui fu incaricato Ando consisteva nel realizzare una galleria per l'esposizione delle ceramiche e dei paraventi giapponesi. Lo spazio è stato diviso in due zone, una delle quali è stata riempita con un reticolo di colonne di trenta centimetri di larghezza e tre metri d'altezza. Queste colonne servono per marcare la profondità dello spazio e generano molteplici vedute, a seconda che si osservino di fronte o di lato. Rievocano, inoltre, lo spirito delle stanze nipponiche dove i sottili montanti di legno e la trasparenza dei paraventi creano degli spazi dinamici, ricchi di giochi di luci ed ombre. Il successo dell'architetto è stato quello di riuscire ad esporre nel modo migliore i paraventi ed, allo stesso tempo, avvolgere l'osservatore in un ambiente tipicamente giapponese.

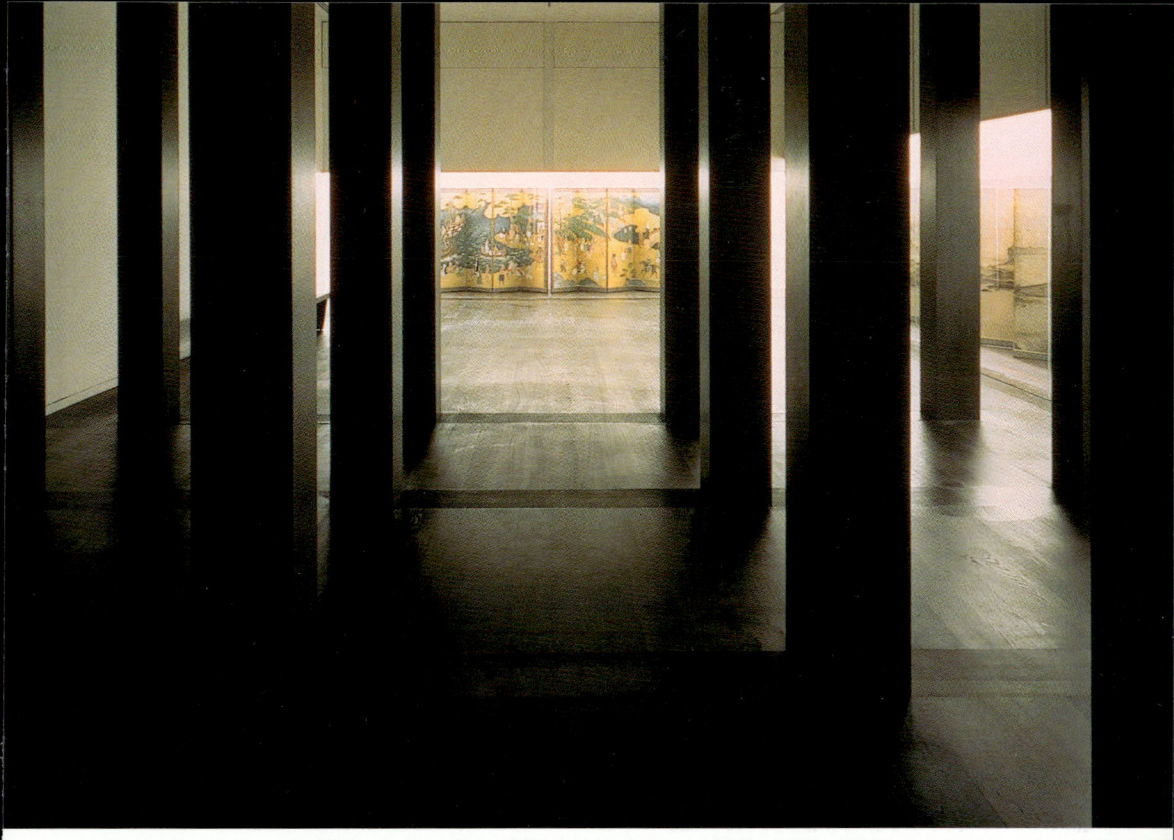

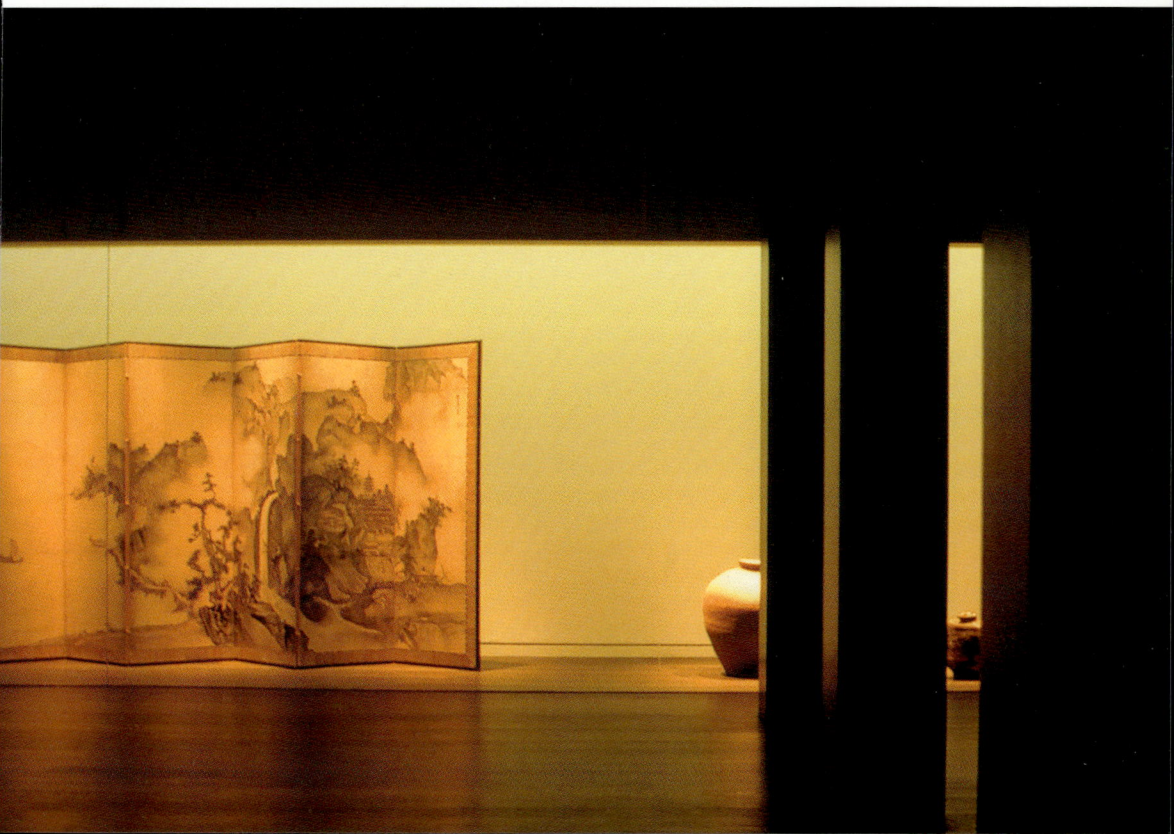

Chikatsu-Asuka Historical Museum

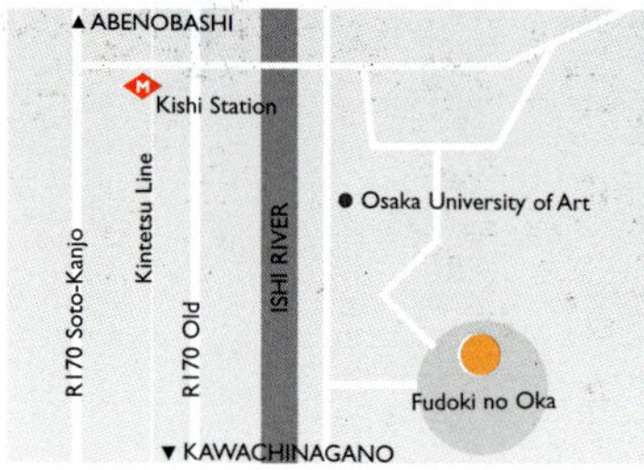

Location: Minamikawachi, Osaka, Japan
Date of construction: 1991–1994
Photographer: Shigeo Ogawa

The zone of Chikatsu-Asuka, south of Osaka prefecture, is the birthplace of the first stage of the history of Japan, characterized by the construction of "kofuns" (burial mounds). In this region is found one of the largest funerary deposits in the country. It contains more than two hundred tombs, four of which are imperial. The museum is dedicated to exhibiting, studying, and providing information about "kofun" culture. It was raised near the excavations on a tumulus that is higher than the rest of the group, as if on a natural hillside. Mounting the large roof stairway, the visitor will begin to make out the tombs as they slowly register on the visual field as a fantastic panorama, completed at the highest point of the perspective. This space is also used for theatrical representations or music festivals. Around the building, plum trees, a pond, and a network of paths around the mounds create a landscape whose cohesion favors open-air activities. The result blends into a cultural and social center that is a veritable reference point in the region. Inside the museum itself, the exhibition spaces are dark; the pieces are displayed as discovered in the tombs.

Das Gebiet von Chikatsu-Asuka im Süden der Präfektur Osaka gilt als die Wiege der Zeit der Kofun Grabhügel aus der frühesten Epoche der japanischen Geschichte. Hier liegt eines der größten Gräberfelder des Landes mit über zweihundert Gräbern, in vieren davon wurden Kaiser bestattet. Das Museum dient der Ausstellung der Funde aus der Kofun-Zeit sowie dem Studium dieser Kultur und der Verbreitung des Wissens darüber. Es wurde in der Nähe der Ausgrabungsstätten auf einem etwas erhöhten Terrain erbaut, so als ob es sich um einen natürlichen Hügel handelte. Wenn man als Besucher die große Freitreppe auf dem Dach emporsteigt, erblickt man nach und nach die Gräber, bis man von ganz oben schließlich einen überwältigenden Rundblick genießt. Hier werden auch Konzerte und Theateraufführungen veranstaltet. Die Landschaft mit ihren Pflaumenbäumen, dem Teich und den Wegen durch die Hügel lädt zu allen erdenklichen Aktivitäten unter freiem Himmel ein und macht den Ort zu einem kulturellen und gesellschaftlichen Zentrum der Region. Die Ausstellungsräume im Inneren des Gebäudes sind dunkel gehalten und die Objekte werden so präsentiert, wie sie einst in den Gräbern gefunden wurden.

La région de Chikatsu-Asuka, au sud de la préfecture d'Osaka, est le berceau de l'ère des « kofuns » (tumulus funéraires), première période de l'histoire du Japon. Elle accueille l'un des plus importants sites funéraires du pays, comprenant plus de deux cents tombes, parmi lesquelles quatre sépultures impériales. Le musée, dédié à l'exposition, à la diffusion et à l'étude de la culture « Kofun », se situe près des fouilles sur le versant le plus élevé de l'ensemble, comme s'il s'agissait d'une colline naturelle. En gravissant le grand toit-gradins, qui accueille, notamment, des représentations théâtrales ou des festivals de musique, le visiteur découvre peu à peu les tombes pour finir par jouir d'un panorama fantastique en atteignant le sommet. Autour de l'édifice, des pruniers, un étang et un réseau de chemins, contournant les monticules, créent un paysage cohérent qui favorise les activités à l'air libre et convertit l'endroit en un centre culturel et social de référence pour la région. À l'intérieur du musée, les espaces d'exposition sont sombres et les pièces présentées en l'état où elles furent découvertes dans les tombes.

La zona di Chikatsu-Asuka, a sud della regione di Osaka, è la culla dell'epoca dei "kofun" (tumuli sepolcrali), prima tappa della storia del Giappone. In questa regione si trova uno dei maggiori giacimenti funerari del paese, che accoglie più di duecento tombe, quattro delle quali sono imperiali. Il museo, che è dedicato all'esposizione, diffusione e studio della cultura "kofun", è situato vicino agli scavi, ad una quota superiore rispetto al complesso, come se si trattasse di una collina naturale. Salendo la grande scalinata d'accesso, il visitatore scorge le tombe poco a poco fino a godere di una fantastica panoramica quando arriva al suo punto più alto. In questo spazio vengono proposte rappresentazioni teatrali e festival di musica. Intorno alla costruzione, i susini, uno stagno ed il reticolo di sentieri che circondano i monticelli creano un paesaggio omogeneo, che favorisce le attività all'aria aperta, e identifica il luogo come un centro culturale e sociale di riferimento per l'intera regione. All'interno del museo, gli spazi d'esposizione sono scuri ed i pezzi vengono esposti così come sono stati ritrovati nelle tombe.

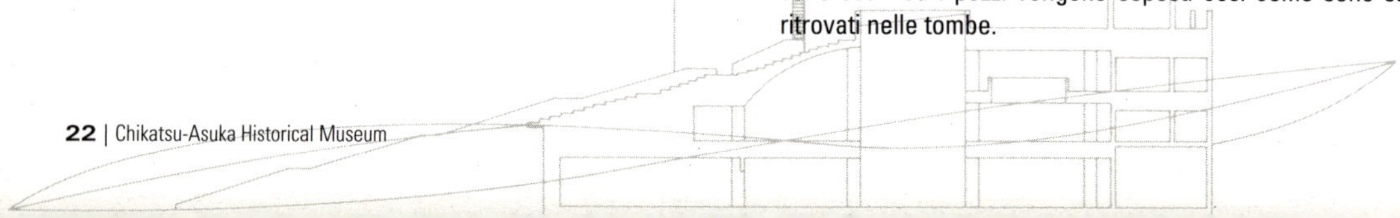

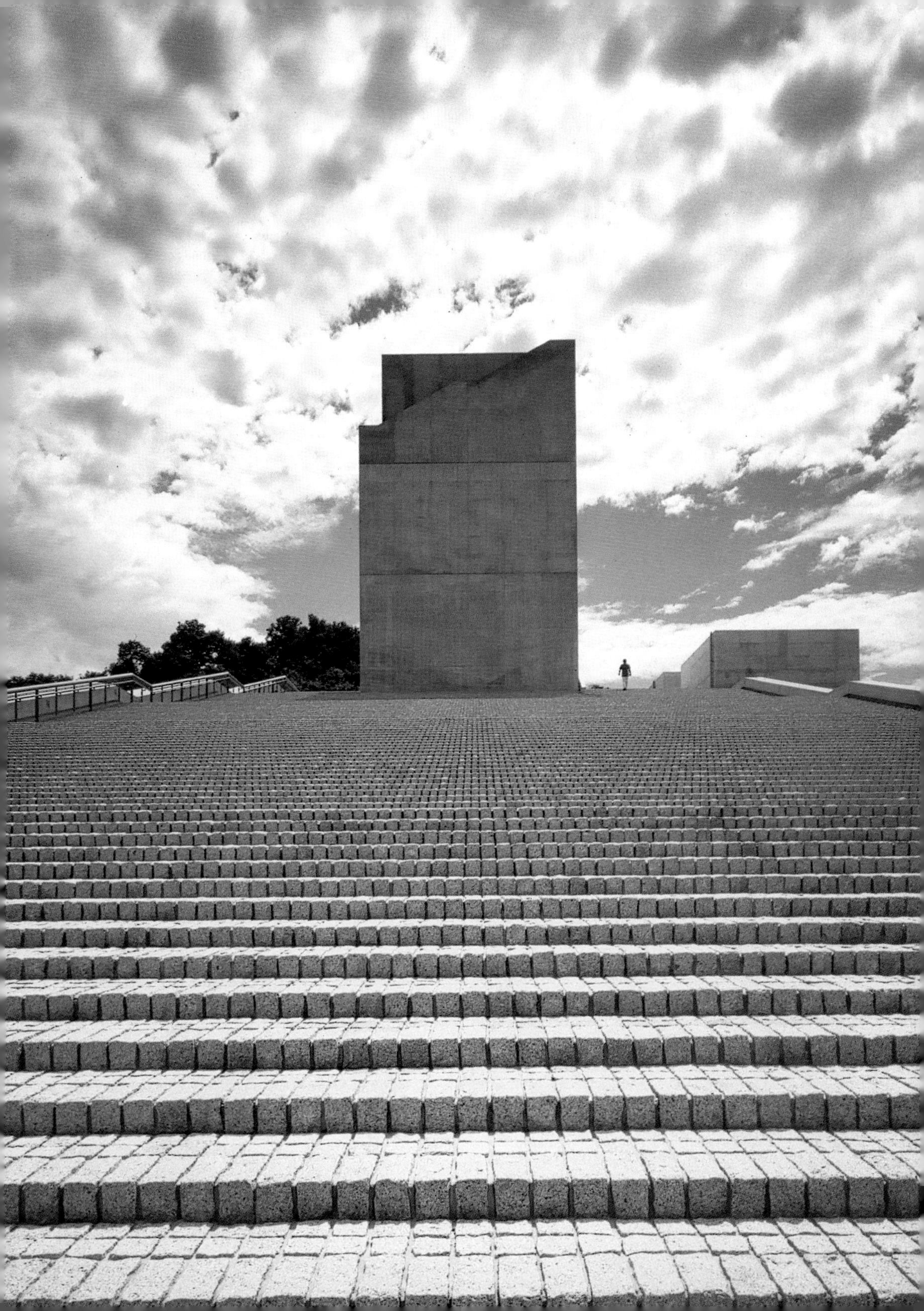

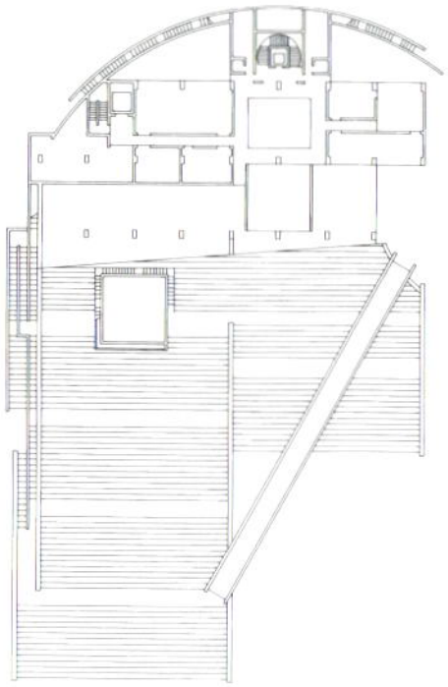

First floor Erstes Obergeschoss
Premier étage **Piano primo**

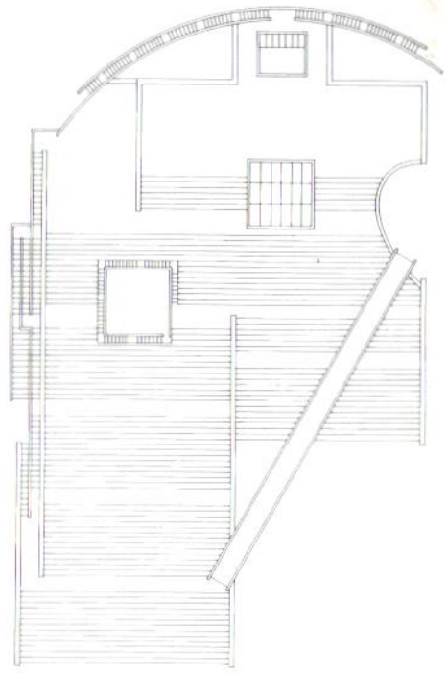

Second floor Zweites Obergeschoss
Deuxième étage **Piano secondo**

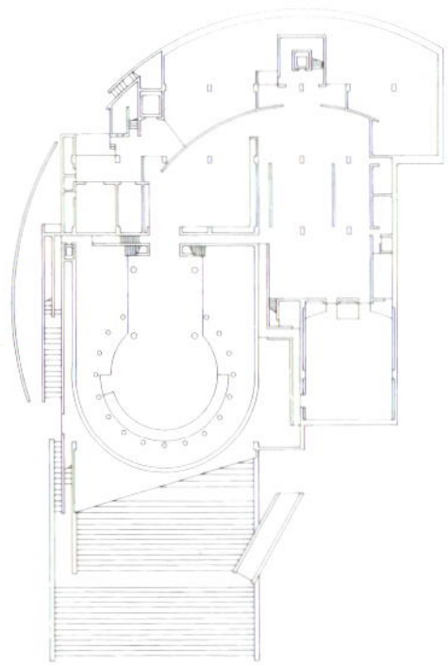

Basement Souterrain
Sous-sol **Piano interrato**

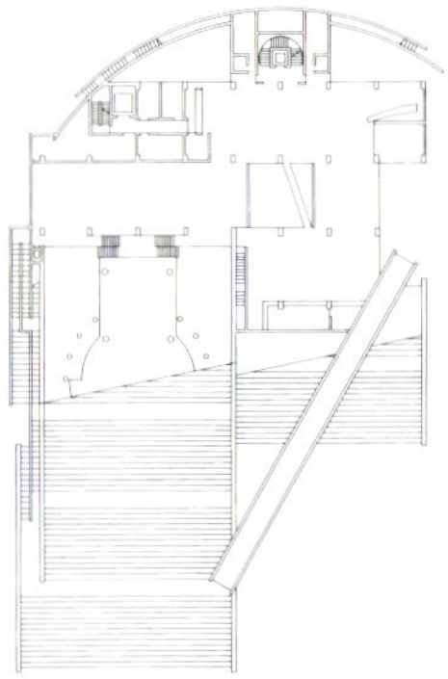

Ground floor Erdgeschoss
Rez-de-chaussée **Piano terra**

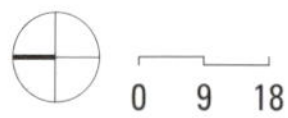

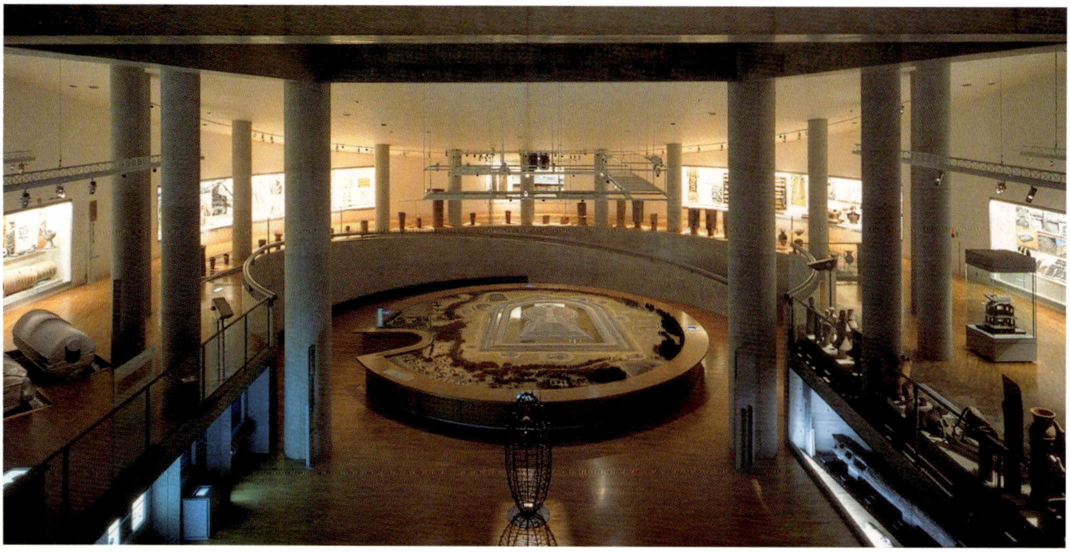

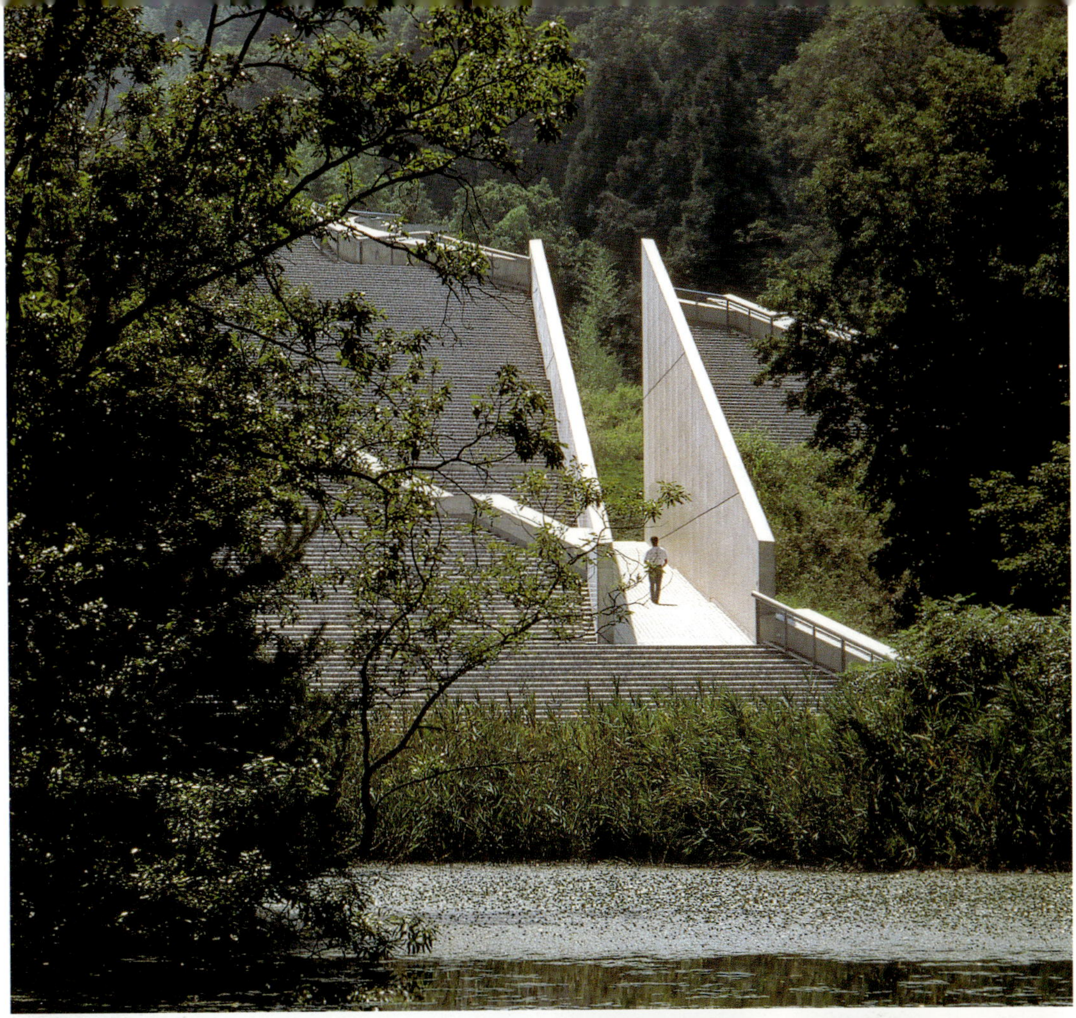

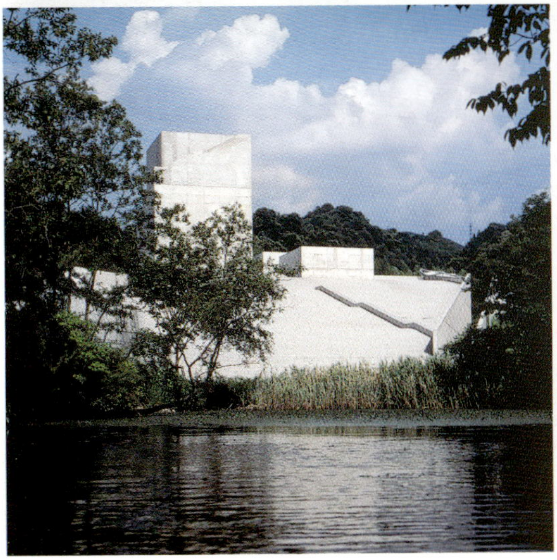

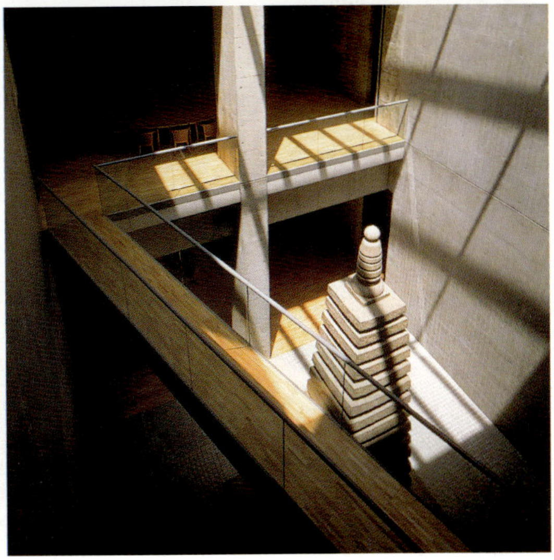

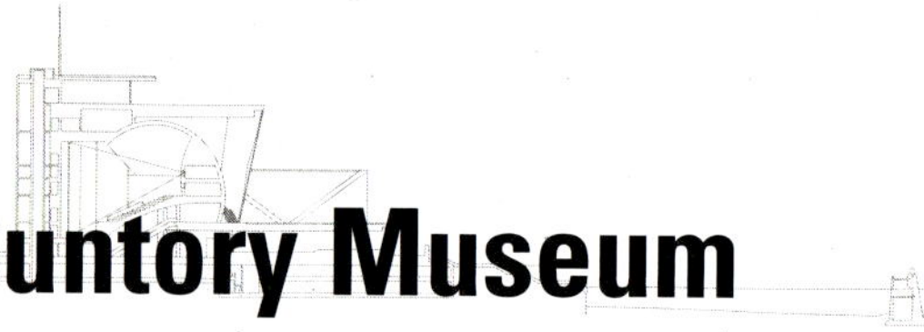

Suntory Museum

Location: Minato, Osaka, Japan
Date of construction: 1992–1994
Photographers: Shigeo Ogawa, Tomio Ohashi

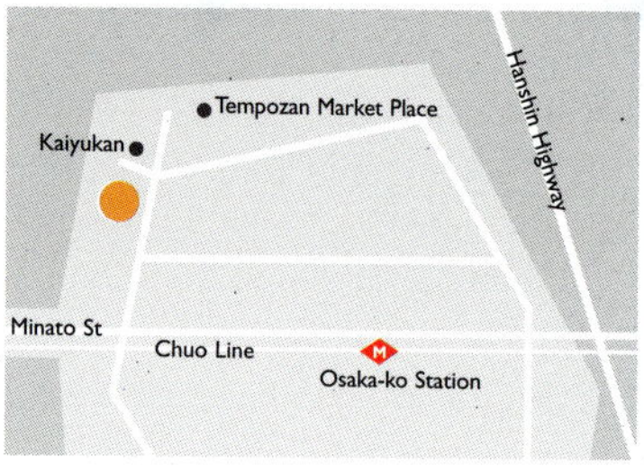

The initial and principal aim of Tadao Ando's project in this museum of fine art was to bring out the richness and value put on water by our contemporary society. The design centers on this fascinating element to draw visitors closer to it as they enter the enclosure via the placement of a square, set right in front of the museum, 100 meters long and 40 meters wide, on the shore of the ocean. This wide public space, shaped by terraces, stairways and slopes and extending to the water itself, can be used as a stage to perform theater plays and concerts. Anyone attending these will also be attending the ocean breeze, the flow of the tides, and the dazzling reflections of the sunlight on the ocean. Water thus becomes still another artwork: Tadao Ando framed it this way. The structural system of the square comprises five columns, and these are repeated in the jetty, some seventy meters from the shore, thus underscoring the continuity between museum and ocean. From the outside, the building is seen as an inverted cone visually sectioned by two rectangular bodies.

Bei diesem Kunstmuseum ging es Tadao Ando vor allem darum, den Wert und die Bedeutung des Wassers für die heutige Gesellschaft herauszustellen. Der Besucher wird über einen Platz an das flüssige Element herangeführt, der vor dem Museum liegt und 100 Meter lang, 40 Meter breit ist und bis direkt ans Ufer des Meeres reicht. Dieser großzügige öffentliche Raum mit seinen Terrassen, Rampen und Freitreppen kann für Theateraufführungen und Konzerte genutzt werden, bei denen die Zuschauer bzw. Zuhörer auch die Meeresbrise, das Kommen und Gehen der Gezeiten und das Glitzern des Sonnenlichts auf dem Ozean genießen können. Das Wasser erscheint selbst wie ein Kunstwerk, das von Tadao Ando eingerahmt und in Szene gesetzt wurde. Auf dem Platz stehen fünf Stelen, die sich als Motiv auf der 70 Meter vor der Küste liegenden Mole wiederholen, wodurch die Kontinuität zwischen Museum und Meer noch stärker betont wird. Der Bau erscheint von außen wie ein umgedrehter Kegel, der von zwei rechteckigen Körpern angeschnitten wird.

L'objectif principal du projet de Tadao Ando pour ce musée d'art était de montrer la richesse et la valeur de l'eau dans la société actuelle. La conception rapproche l'élément des visiteurs de l'enceinte à l'aide d'une place: devant le musée, de 100 mètres de long pour 40 mètres de large, elle descend jusqu'au bord de la mer. Ce grand espace public, formé par des terrasses, des escaliers et des rampes menant à l'eau, peut servir de scène pour des représentations théâtrales ou des concerts. Il devient ainsi possible de jouir de la brise marine, du mouvement des marées et des reflets du soleil dans l'océan. L'eau est traitée comme une œuvre d'art additionnelle et Tadao Ando l'a « cadrée ». La structure de la place inclu une rangée de cinq piliers se répétant sur la jetée, à quelques soixante-dix mètres de la rive, soulignant ainsi la continuité entre le musée et la mer. Depuis l'extérieur, le bâtiment présente un volume conique inversé, sectionnée par deux corps rectangulaires.

L'obiettivo principale del progetto di Tadao Ando per questo museo d'arte era mostrare la ricchezza ed il valore dell'acqua nella società attuale. Il progetto avvicina quest'elemento ai visitatori del museo mediante la costruzione di una piazza ubicata davanti al museo, di 100 metri di lunghezza e 40 di larghezza, fino in riva al mare. Questo grande spazio pubblico, formato da terraze, scalinate e rampe che arrivano fino all'acqua, può essere utilizzato come scenario per opere teatrali e concerti durante i quali si può godere la brezza marina, il movimento delle maree ed il riflesso del sole sull'oceano. È l'acqua stessa che diventa un'opera d'arte e Tadao Ando la tratta come tale. La piazza contiene cinque colonne che si ripetono anche su la diga, a circa settanta metri dalla riva, il che enfatizza la continuità tra il museo ed il mare. All'esterno l'edificio si presenta come un cono rovesciato, sezionato da due corpi rettangolari.

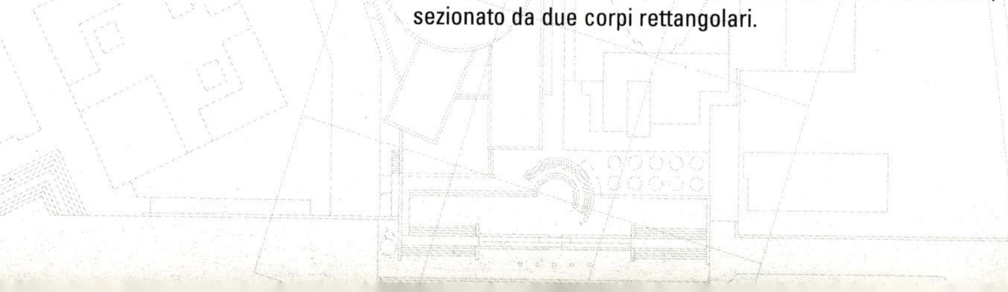

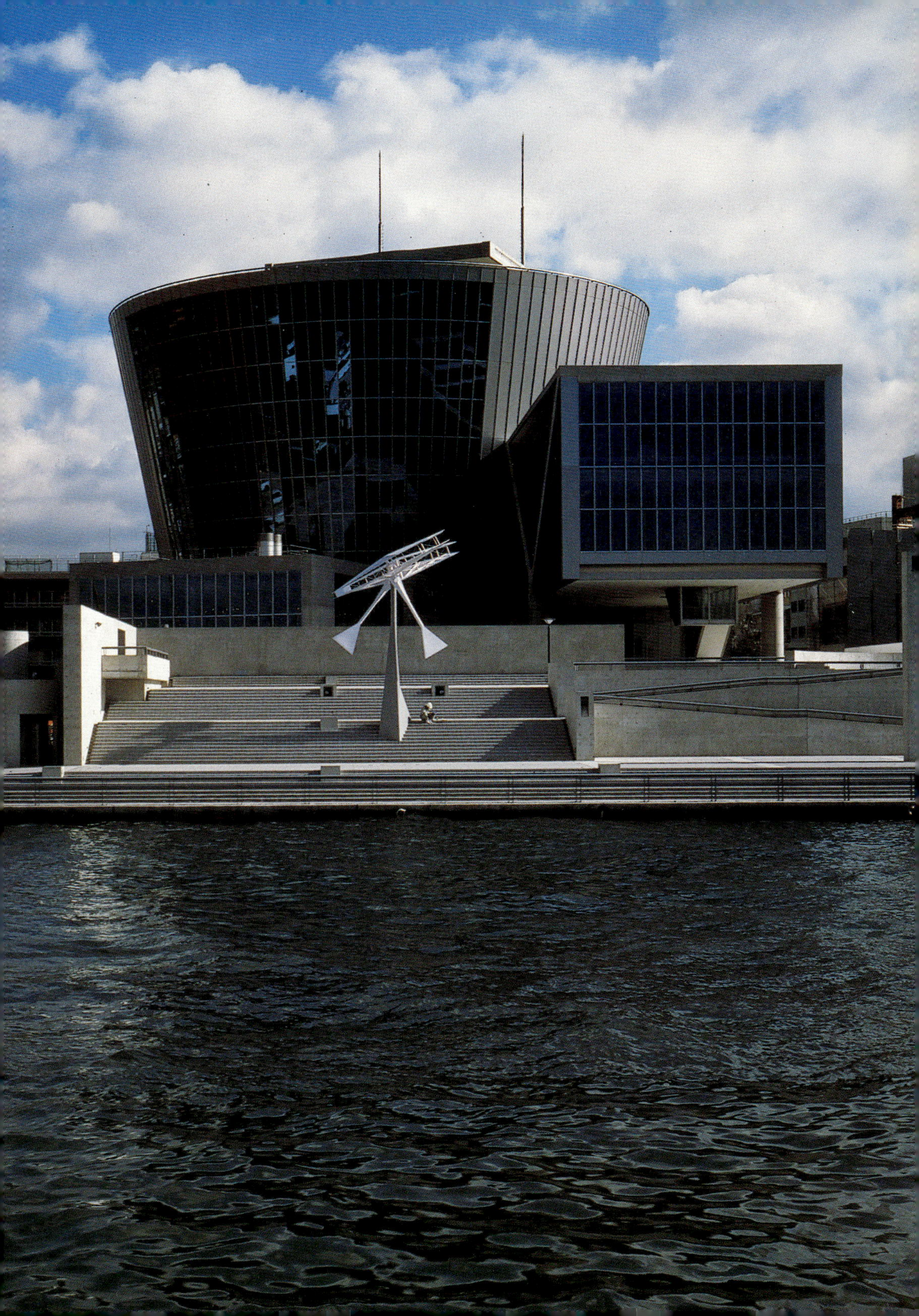

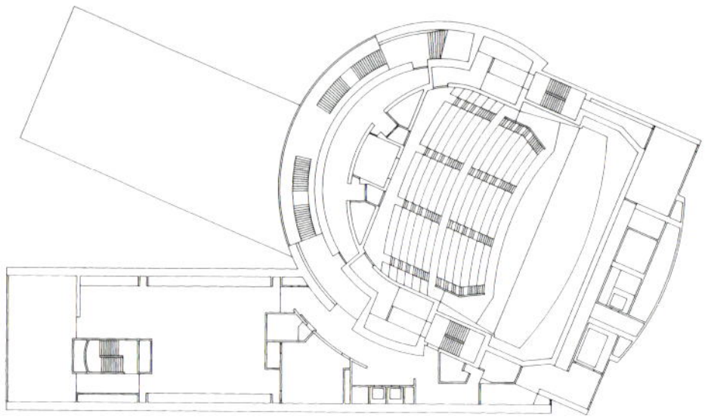

Sixth floor Sixième étage

Sechstes Obergeschoss **Piano sesto**

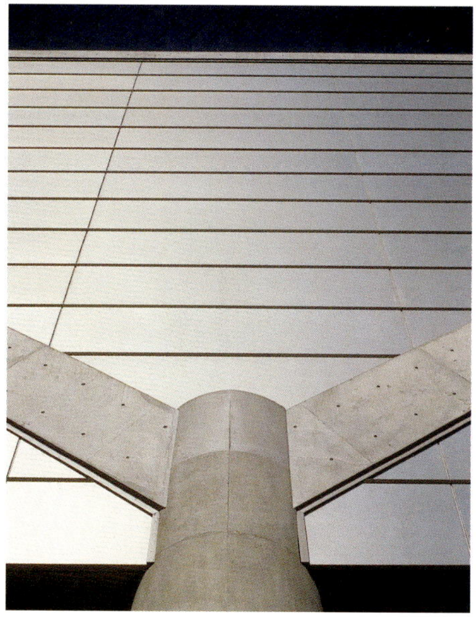

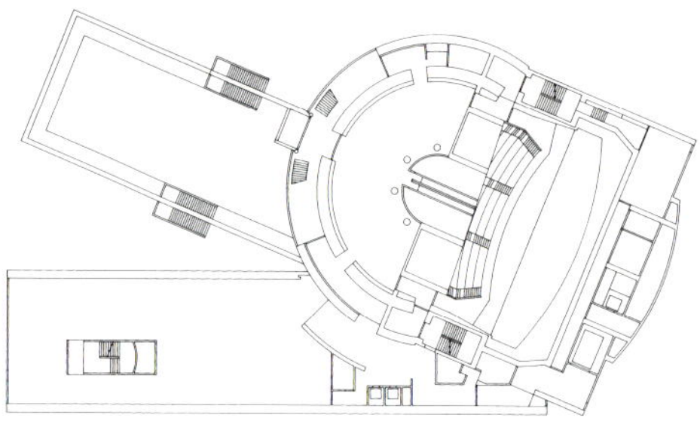

Fifth floor Cinquième étage

Fünftes Obergeschoss **Piano quinto**

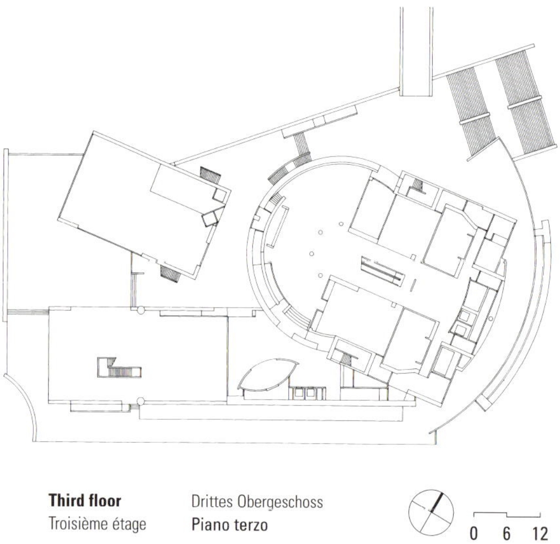

Third floor Troisième étage

Drittes Obergeschoss **Piano terzo**

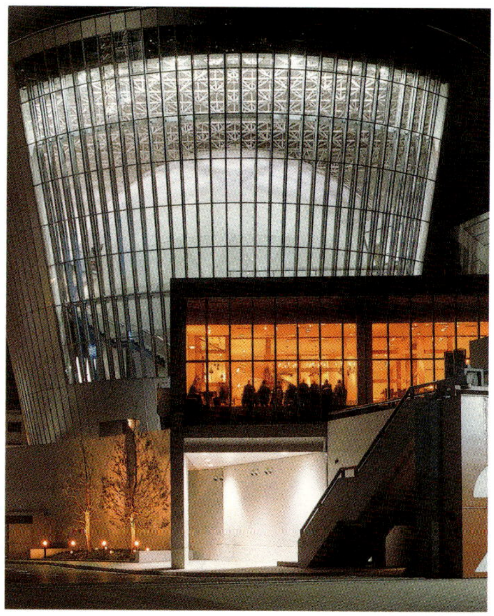

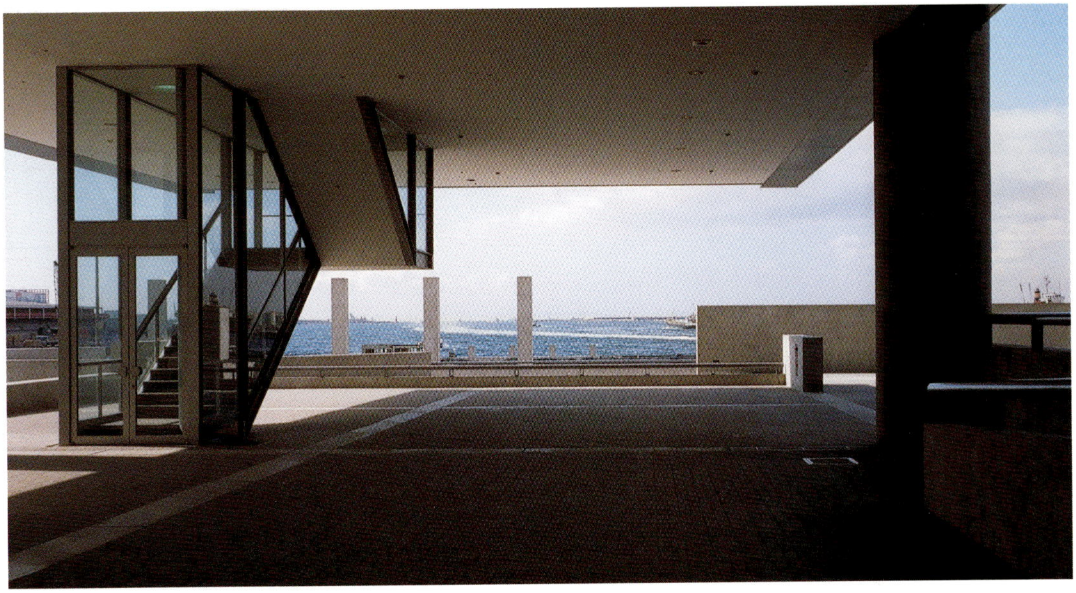

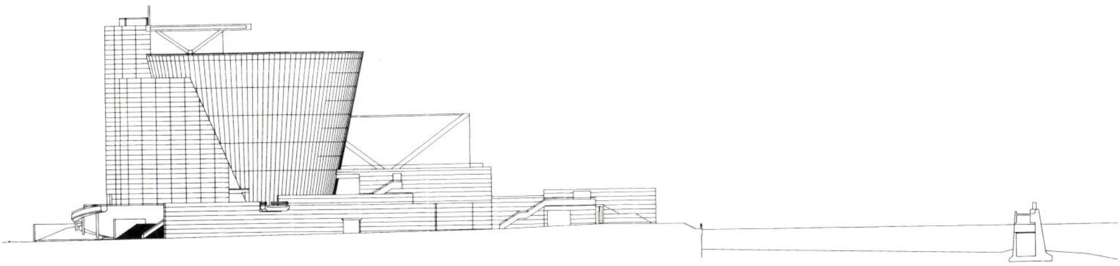

Elevation Aufriss
Elévation **Prospetto**

0 8 16

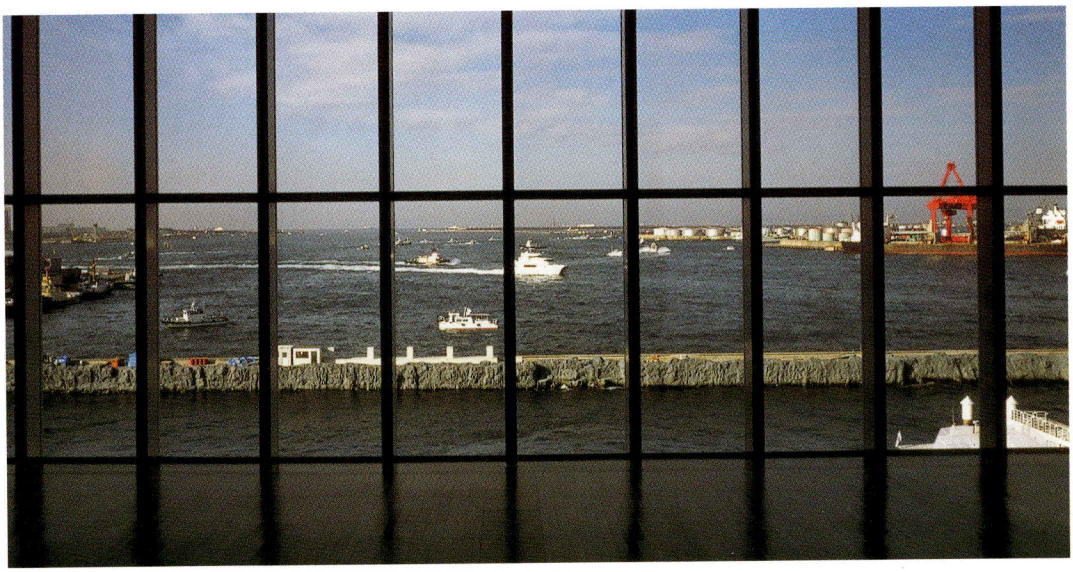

Museum of Wood

Location: Mikata, Hyogo, Japan
Date of construction: 1993–1994
Photographers: Mitsuo Matsuoka, Shigeo Ogawa

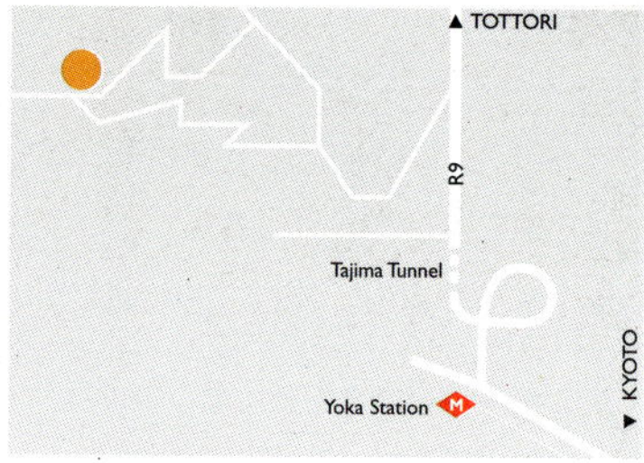

The progressive deterioration of the environment has been for Tadao Ando the wherefore to develop an architecture respecting of ecosystems, one which induces its users to reflect on their ecological actions. This mode is seen very acutely in projects like the Museum of Wood. Here, it was necessary to carry out a profound recognition of the settings in order to reveal a complex that reads nature attentively and is capable of yielding a new vision, a new appreciation of the woodlands. The work is located in a zone of lush vegetation, and this fact makes it conducive to a priority of searching for a strategic arrangement of the building, one gauged to avoid any unnecessary felling of trees. This museum is on a circular plan 46 meters in diameter and 18 meters tall. In its large room, objects related to culture, industry, and woodworking are on display. A helicoidal ramp runs around the inside perimeter and a catwalk crosses the space to access the annex. In the open-air center there is a pond which makes the visual effect of sky and water a powerful one.

Die stetig zunehmende Umweltzerstörung war für Tadao Ando Anlass, eine umweltverträgliche Architektur zu entwickeln, die die Menschen zum Nachdenken über ökologische Probleme anregt. Besonders augenfällig wird dieser Ansatz des Architekten in einem Projekt wie dem Holzmuseum. Der Bauplatz musste genauestens studiert werden, um einen Bau zu errichten, der mit der Natur in Einklang steht und eine neue Sicht auf den Wald anregt. Der Komplex liegt in einer dicht bewaldeten Gegend, weshalb versucht wurde, ihn so auszurichten, dass möglichst wenige Bäume gefällt werden mussten. Das Museum erhebt sich 18 Meter hoch auf einem kreisförmigen Grundriss von 46 Metern Durchmesser. In der einzelner Halle werden Exponate ausgestellt, die mit der Kultur des Holzes, der Holzindustrie und dem Kunsthandwerk in Beziehung stehen. Eine spiralförmige Rampe führt im Inneren nach oben und ein quer durch diesen Innenhof führender Steg verbindet den Hauptbau mit einem abseits gelegenen Nebengebäude. Im Zentrum des nach oben offenen Rundbaus liegt ein Wasserbecken, in dem sich der Himmel effektvoll spiegelt.

La détérioration croissante de l'environnement a conduit Tadao Ando à développer une architecture respectueuse de l'écosystème et suscitant la réflexion écologique de ses usagers. Cette tendance s'accentue pour des projets tel le Musée du Bois, nécessitant une reconnaissance profonde de l'environnement afin de projeter un complexe attentif à la nature et à même d'offrir une nouvelle vision, une nouvelle appréciation de la forêt. L'œuvre est située dans une zone à la végétation luxuriante. De là une priorité donnée à la recherche d'une implantation stratégique de la construction, afin d'éviter la coupe inutile d'arbres. Le musée repose sur un unique niveau circulaire de 46 mètres de diamètre et de 18 mètres de haut. Cette grande salle permet l'exposition d'objets en relation avec la culture, l'industrie et l'artisanat du bois. Une rampe hélicoïdale parcourt son périmètre intérieur et une passerelle traverse l'espace pour accéder à une annexe. De plus, au centre, en plain air est installé un étang offrant une rencontre visuelle puissante entre l'eau et le ciel.

Il crescente degrado dell'ambiente ha portato Tadao Ando a sviluppare un'architettura rispettosa dell'ecosistema e che induce i suoi utenti ad una riflessione ecologica. Questa tendenza si vede rafforzata in progetti come il Museo del Legno, dove si doveva portare a termine un profondo esame della zona per progettare un complesso attento alla natura e che fosse capace di dare una visione nuova, una nuova valorizzazione dei boschi. L'opera è situata in una zona ricca di vegetazione, fatto che ha favorito la ricerca di una disposizione strategica dell'edificio per evitare l'abbattimento inutile di alberi. Il museo ha una planimetria circolare di 46 metri di diametro e 18 metri d'altezza. In questa grande sala sono esposti oggetti che sono in relazione con la cultura, l'industria e l'artigianato del legno. Una rampa elicoidale percorre il suo perimetro interno ed una passerella incrocia lo spazio per accedere all'edificio annesso. Al centro, all'aria aperta, è stato sistemato uno stagno che offre un potente effetto visivo nell'incontro tra acqua e cielo.

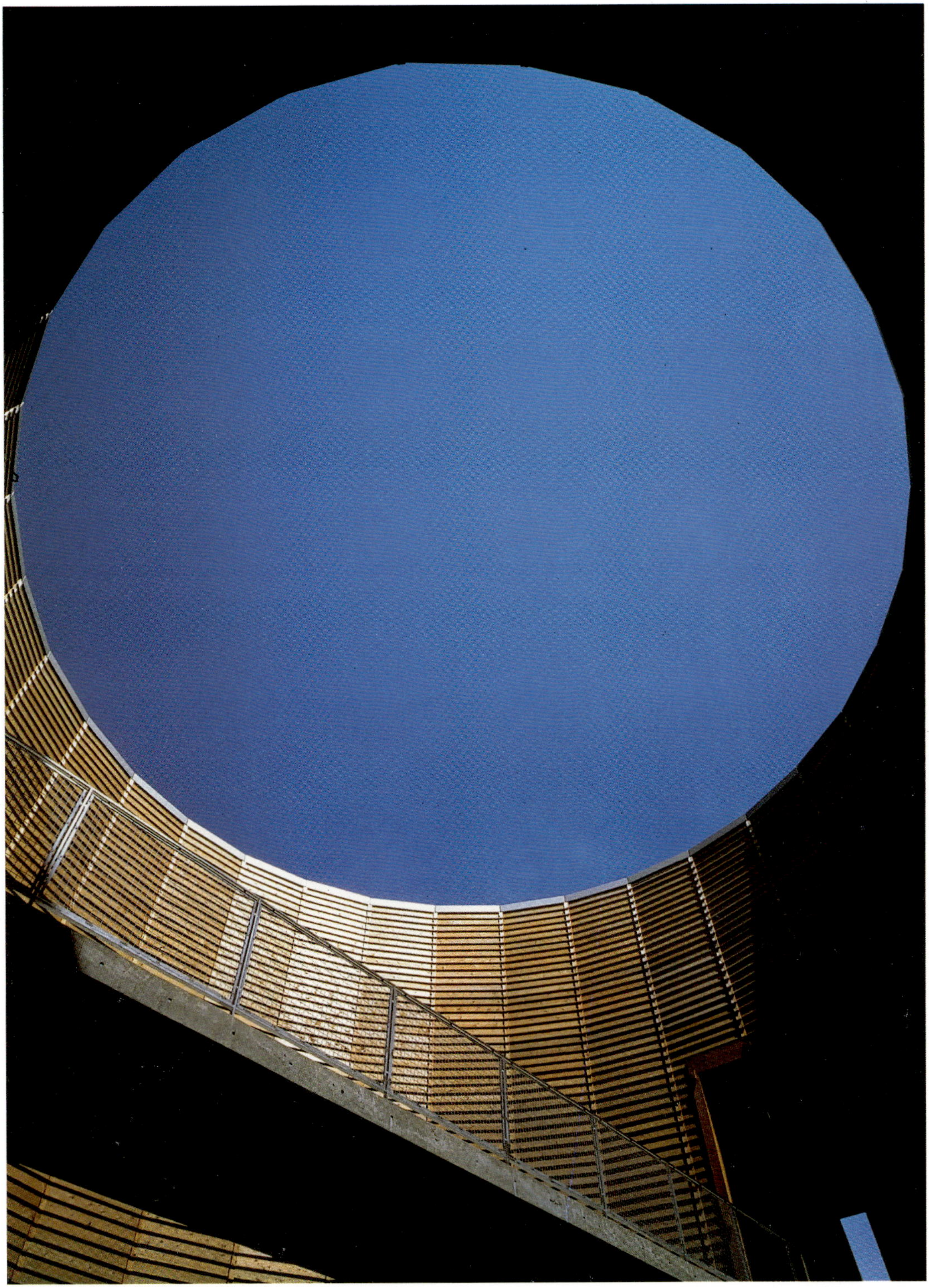

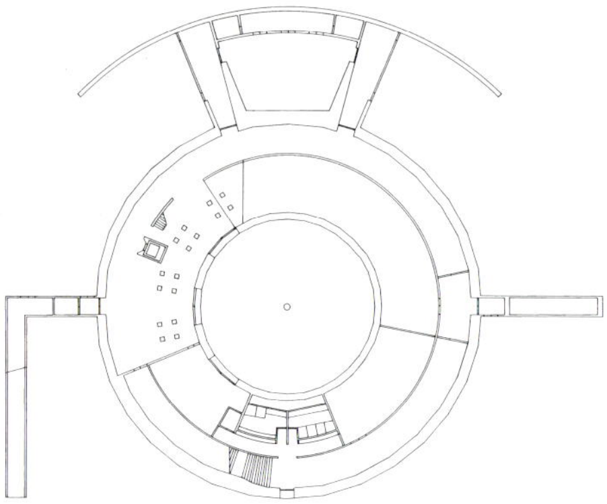

Ground floor Erdgeschoss
Rez-de-chaussée **Piano terra**

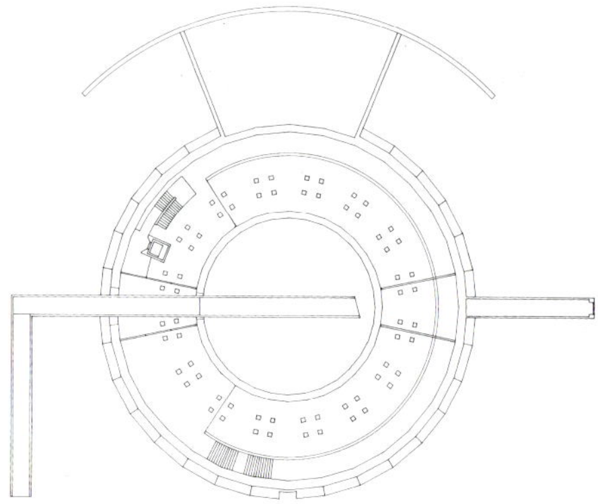

First floor Erstes Obergeschoss
Premier étage **Piano primo**

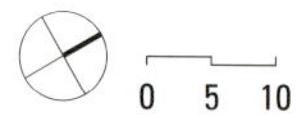

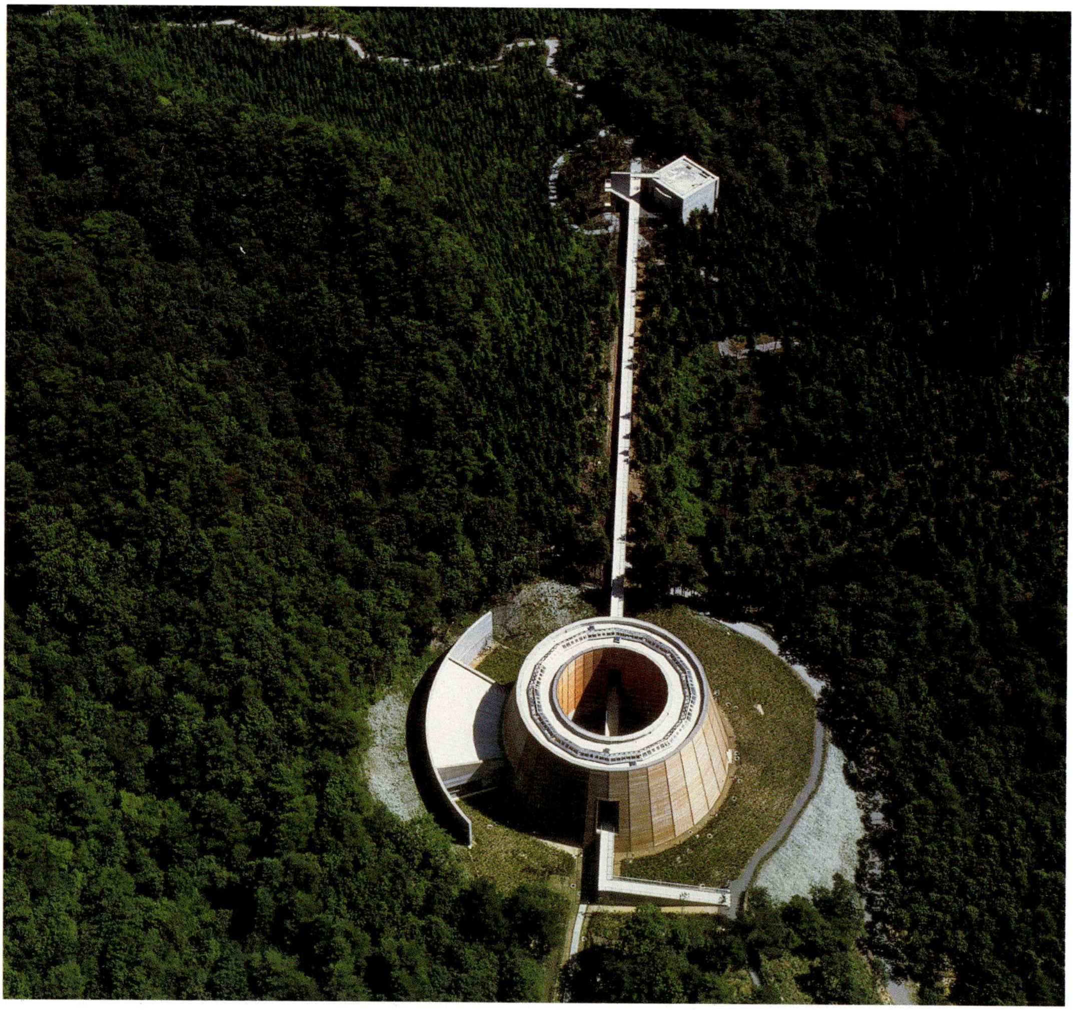

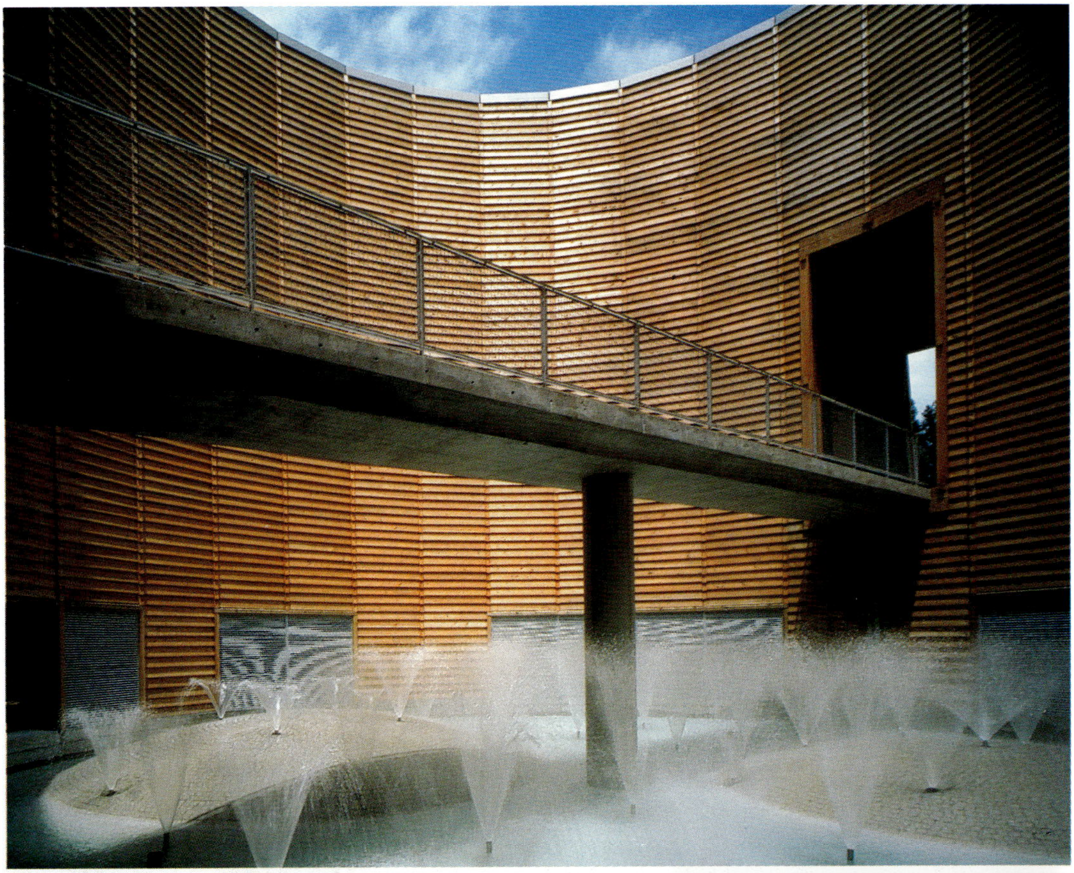

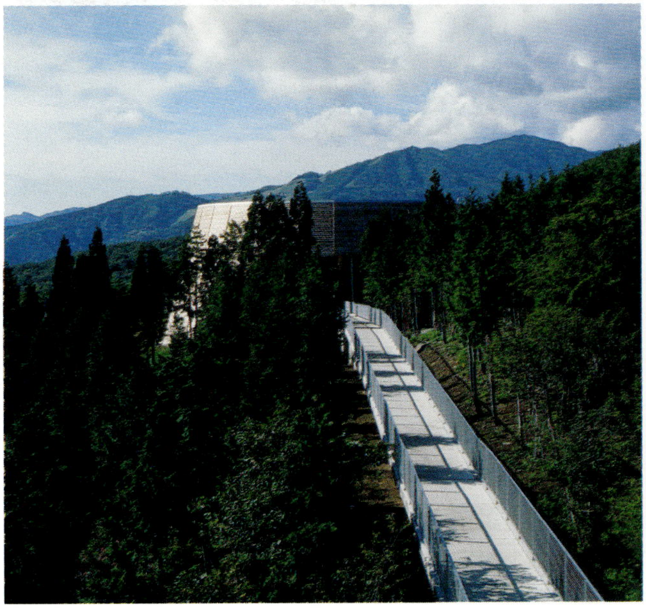

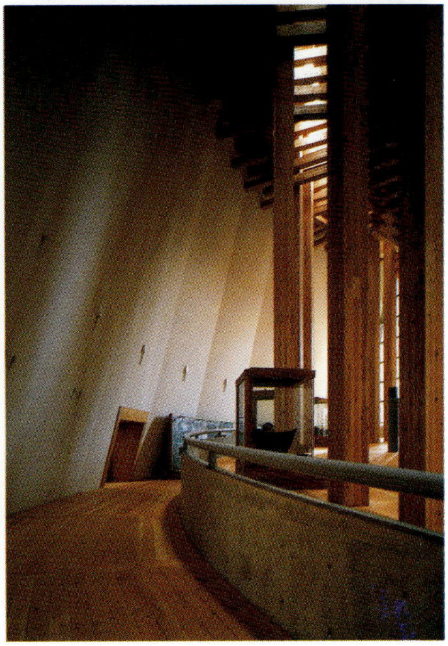

Nariwa Museum

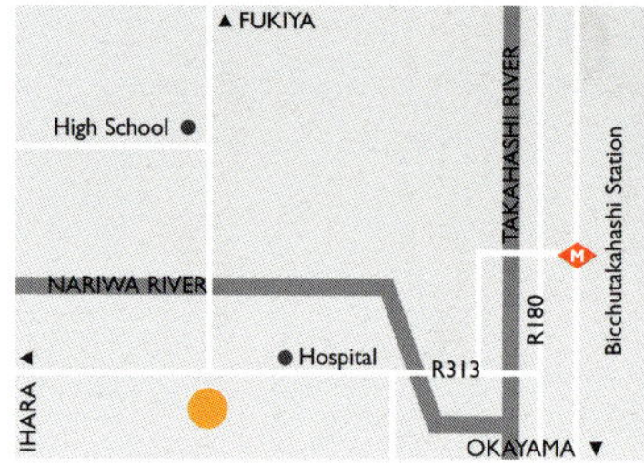

Location: Kawakami, Okayama, Japan
Date of construction: 1993–1994
Photographers: Mitsuo Matsuoka, Shigeo Ogawa

Nariwa, in Okayama prefecture, in western Japan, is a financially prosperous place whose wealth comes from the copper mining industry. Culturally, also, it is rich because it is the site of many traditional houses, called "fukiya", buildings whose façades are colored in a distinctive reddish tone. This art museum is on the site of old residences, surrounded by a stone wall and limited on the south by a steep grade. The project is expressed in the form of a new perimeter wall containing a concrete edifice in which the different museum functions take place. Between the slanted plane and the building itself, a wide sheet of water reflects Ando's "fukiya" poem. Go up to this museum and you first find the old stone wall, a witness to the past. The next step is the ramp leading to the path that goes around the construction. It all becomes a place that fuses nature, culture, history. And in its interior vertical slabs of concrete merge with a large-scale glass cladding that fills the museum with diffuse light and offers magnificent views of the surrounding landscape.

Nariwa in der westjapanischen Präfektur von Okayama ist dank des Kupferbergbaus eine wirtschaftlich prosperierende Stadt, die auch in kultureller Hinsicht privilegiert ist, da sich dort zahlreiche traditionelle „Fukiya"-Häuser finden, deren Fassaden in verschiedenen Rottönen gestrichen sind. Dieses Kunstmuseum befindet sich auf dem Gelände alten Anwesens. Es ist von einer Steinmauer umgeben und grenzt im Süden an einen steilen Abhang. Der Entwurf sah eine neue Mauer vor, die die Betonstruktur umgibt, in der die verschiedenen Einrichtungen des Museums untergebracht sind. Zwischen dem Abhang und dem Gebäude erstreckt sich eine weitläufige Wasserfläche, in der sich die Schönheit des Baus spiegelt. Die Besucher des Museums treffen zuerst auf eine alte Steinmauer, eine Reminiszenz der Vergangenheit, und werden anschließend über eine Rampe auf einen Weg geleitet, der um das Gelände herumführt. Die Anlage wird so zu einem Ort, an dem Natur, Kultur und Geschichte miteinander verschmelzen. Im Inneren wechseln senkrechte Betonflächen mit großen Glasfens-tern ab, die die Räume mit diffusem Licht erfüllen und zugleich herrliche Ausblicke auf die Landschaft erlauben.

Nariwa, dans la préfecture d'Okayama, à l'ouest du Japon, est une localité à l'économie prospère grâce à l'industrie minière du cuivre. Sa richesse culturelle tient, elle, aux nombreuses maisons traditionnelles, nommées « fukiya », aux façades colorées d'un ton rougeâtre distinctif. Ce musée d'art est situé sur le terrain d'anciennes résidences, enceint d'un mur de pierre et limité au sud par une pente prononcée. Le projet comprend un nouveau mur d'enceinte autour d'un volume de béton qui accueille les diverses fonctions du musée. Entre la pente et l'édifice, un grand plan d'eau reflète la poésie de l'œuvre. Les visiteurs s'approchant du musée découvrent d'abord l'ancien mur de pierre, témoin du passé. Puis ils gravissent une rampe qui les conduit le long d'une promenade contournant la construction. L'enceinte se convertit ainsi en un lieu où fusionnent la nature, la culture et l'histoire. À l'intérieur, les pans verticaux de béton se combinent avec les grandes façades vitrées inondant les intérieurs de lumière diffuse, tout en offrant des vues splendides sur le paysage alentour.

Nariwa, situata nella regione di Okayama, nella parte occidentale del Giappone, è una località economicamente prospera, grazie all'industria mineraria del rame, e ricca culturalmente perché ospita numerose case tradizionali chiamate "fukiya", le cui facciate sono tinteggiate di un caratteristico colore rossiccio. Questo museo dell'arte è situato sul terreno di antiche residenze, circondato da un muro di pietra e limitato a sud da un accentuato pendio. Il progetto consiste in un nuovo muro di contenimento nel quale si inserisce una costruzione di cemento armato che accoglie le diverse funzionalità del museo. Tra il pendio e l'edificio una grande lamina d'acqua riflette la poesia dell'opera. I visitatori che si avvicinano al museo incontrano prima l'antico muro di pietra, testimone del passato, poi salgono per una rampa che li conduce lungo una passeggiata che circonda la costruzione. L'intera struttura si trasforma così in un luogo dove si fondono natura, cultura e storia. All'interno, i piani verticali di cemento sono affiancati a grandi vetrate che inondano di luce diffusa l'interno, ed offrono, allo stesso tempo, splendide panoramiche sul paesaggio circostante.

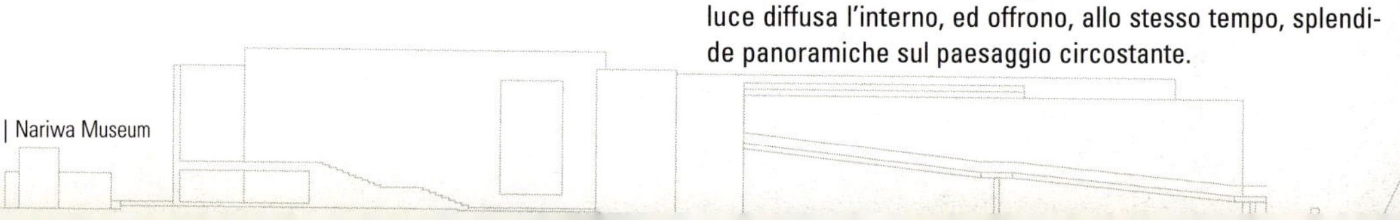

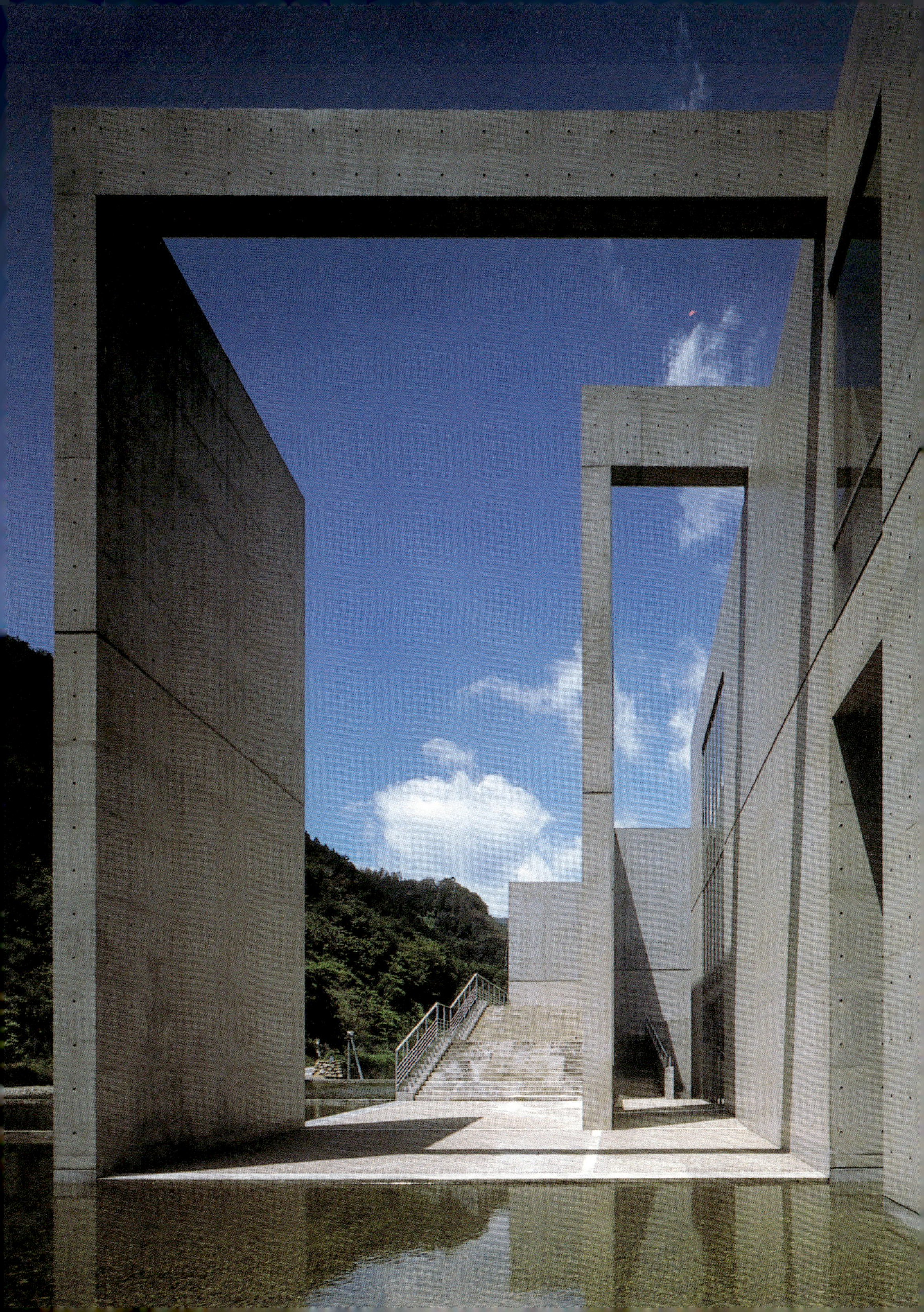

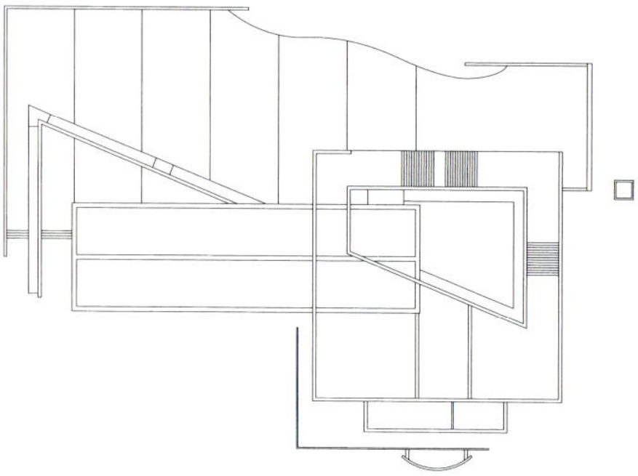

Roof plan Grundriss der Dächer
Niveau supérieur **Pianta delle coperture**

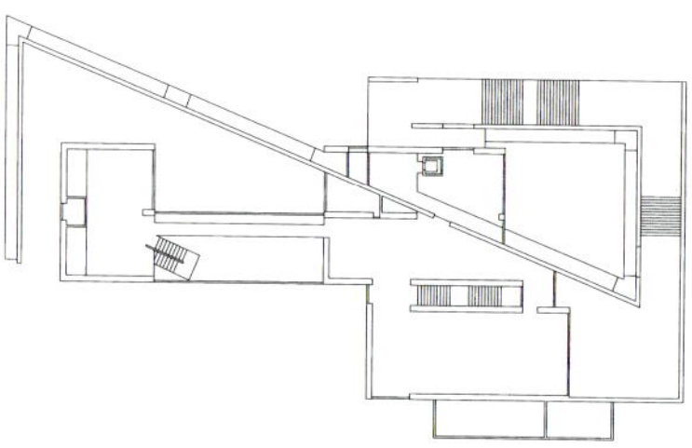

First floor Erstes Obergeschoss
Premier étage **Piano primo**

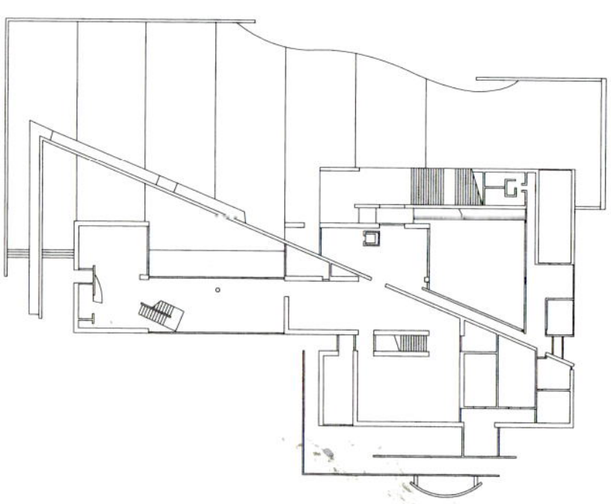

Ground floor Erdgeschoss
Rez-de-chaussée **Piano terra**

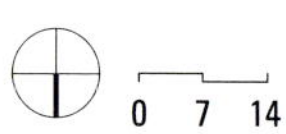

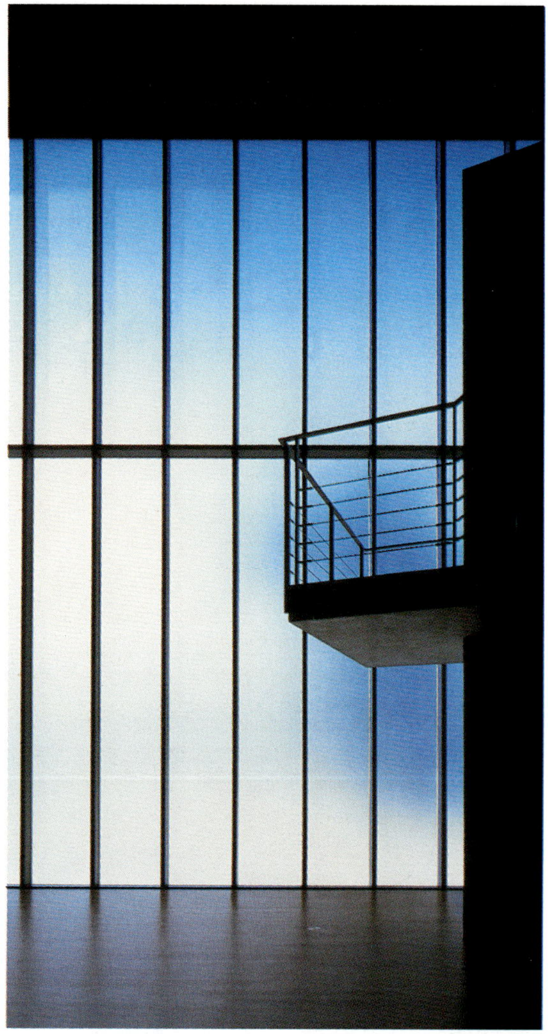

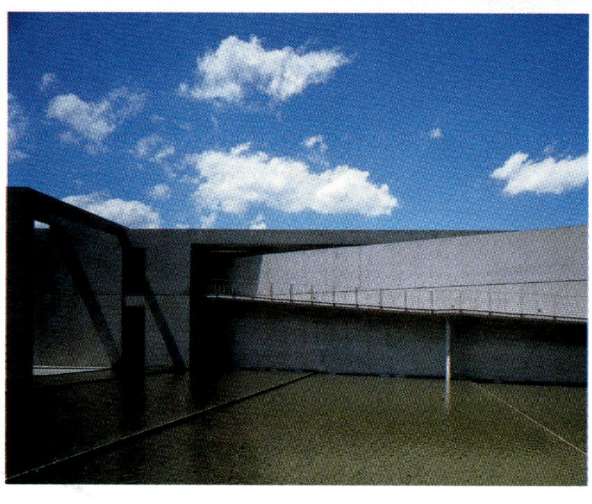

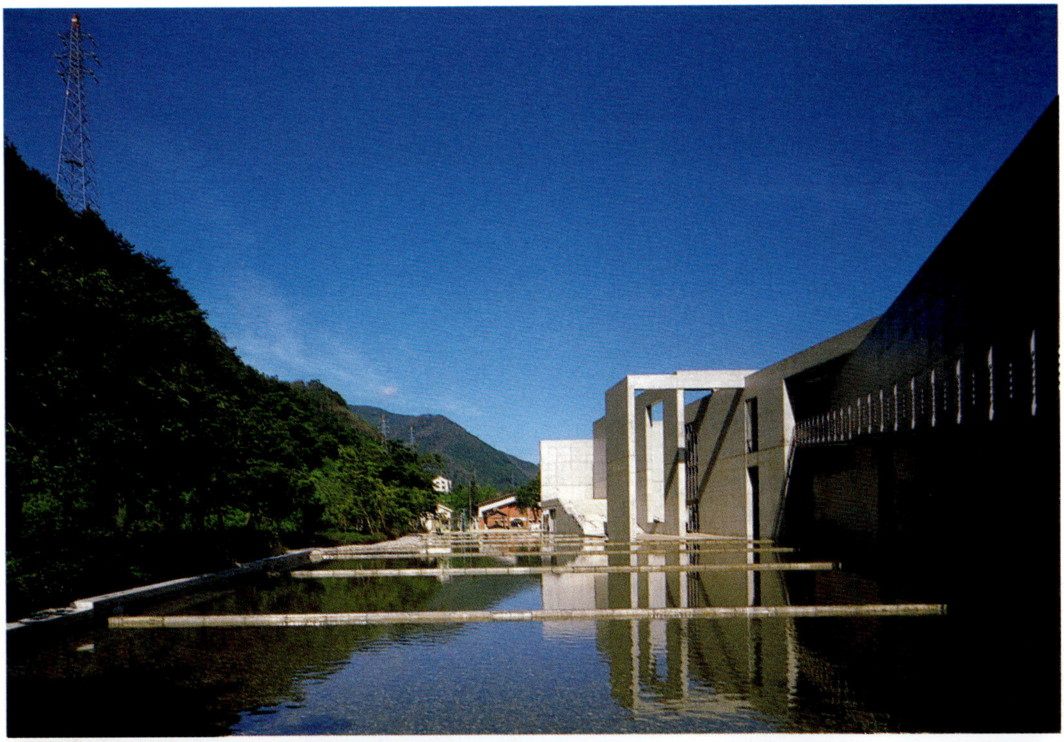

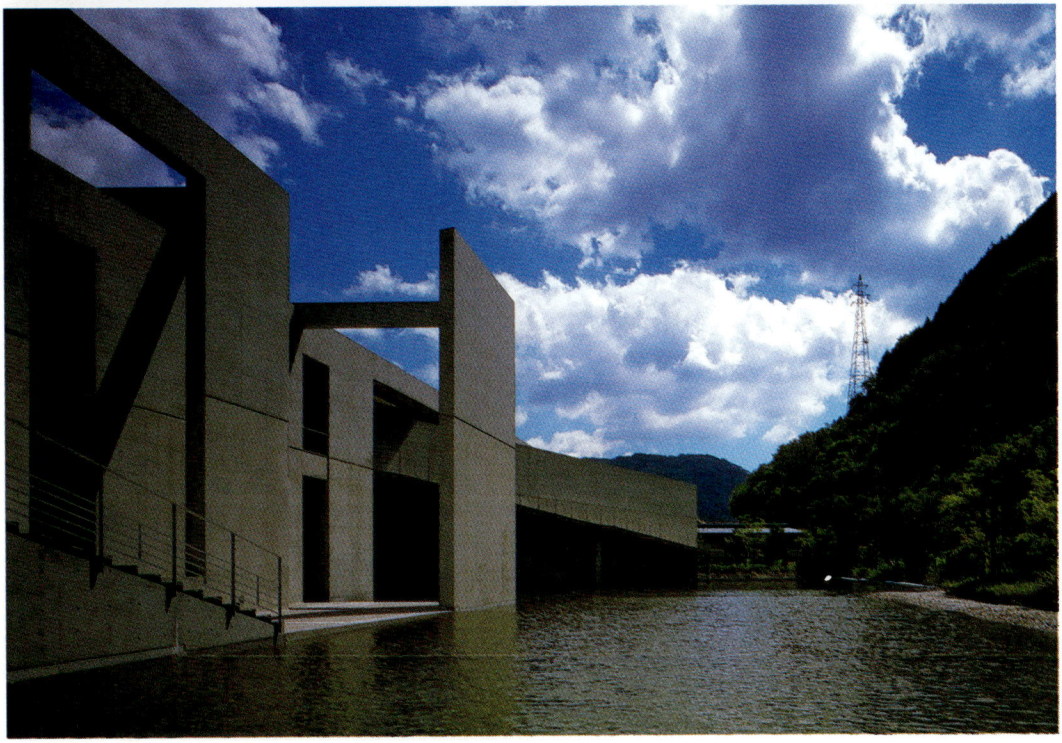

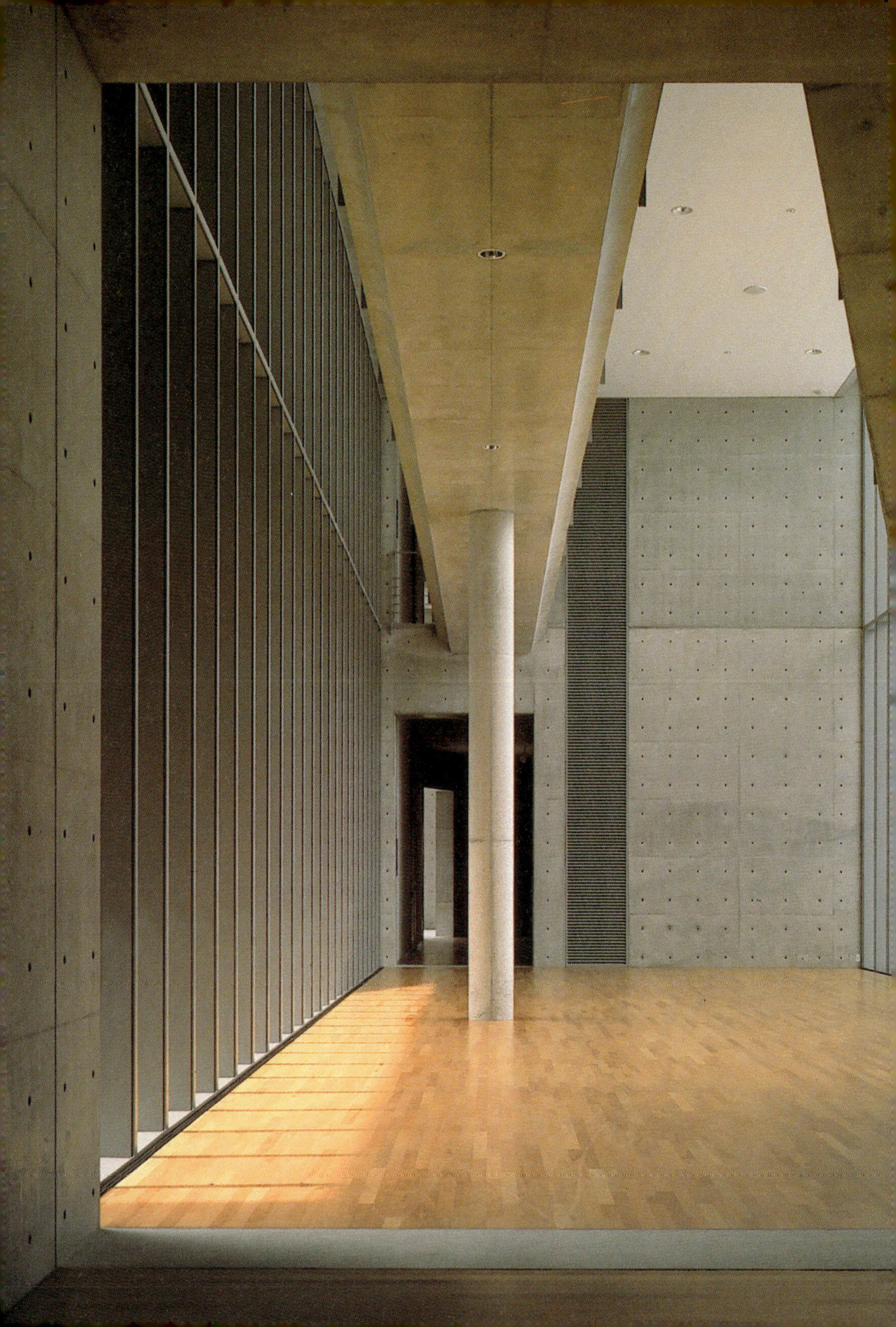

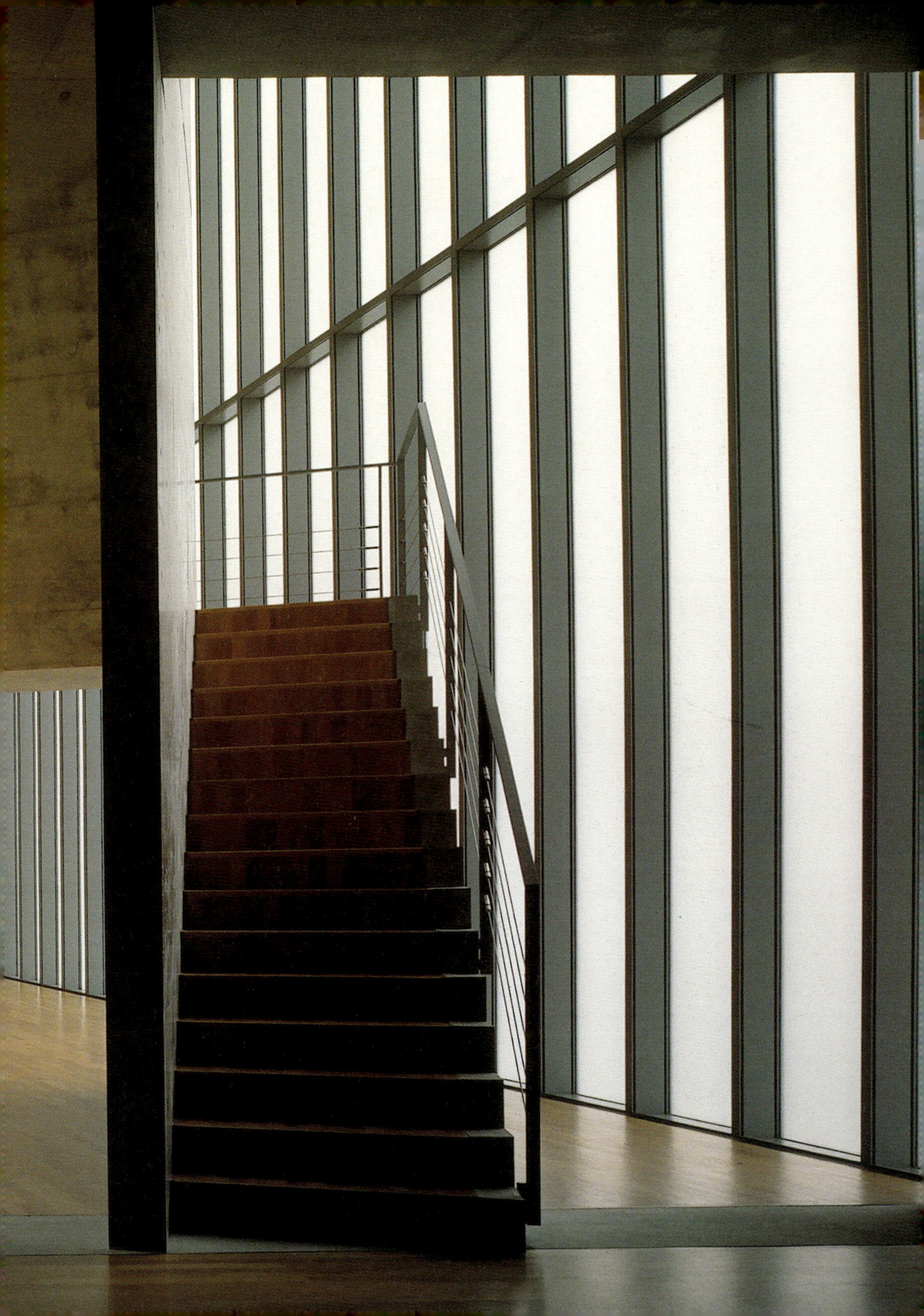

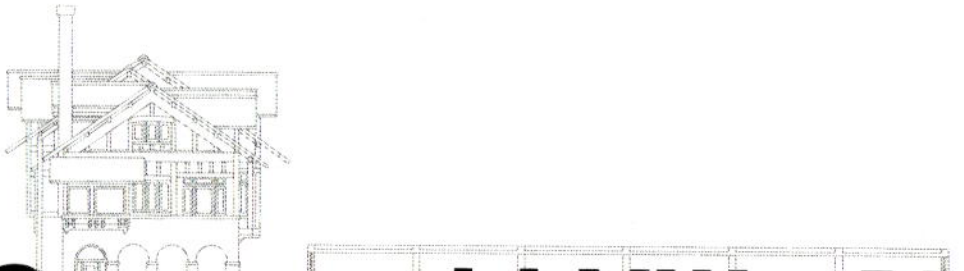

Oyamazaki Villa Museum

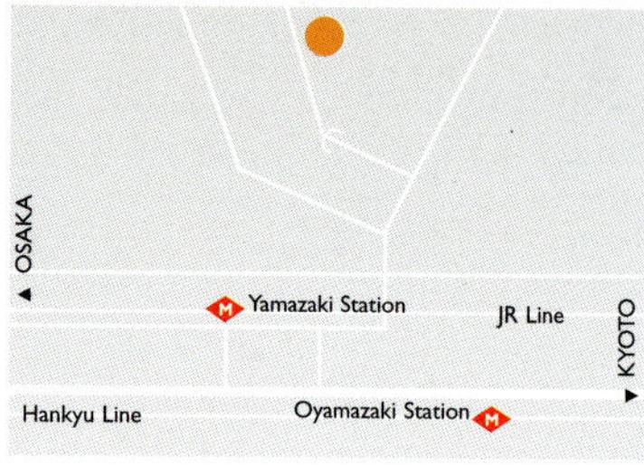

Location: Oyamazaki, Kyoto, Japan
Date of construction: 1994–1995
Photographer: Mitsuo Matsuoka

Doing this project meant providing a 1920s house with the necessary infrastructures to be used as an art museum. In spite of the fact that the existing building had been raised at a time when Western influences scarcely existed in Japanese architecture, the owner took inspiration from buildings of the Tudor style seen while studying in Britain. Tadao Ando was aiming for a stimulating interaction between this architecture characterized by its expressive details and modern open space. Along with the original structure, a cylindrical gallery six meters in diameter was put up. It was partially sunk into the terrain in order to avoid blocking the view of the old building and of the garden. To accompany this new structure, vegetation was planted on the roof and around the new cylinder to assure harmonious blending with the original setting. The two buildings, independent, autonomous, interface by way of stairs to offer highly distinct spatial experiences. The old houses a full collection of ceramics; the new shows important Impressionist pieces such as one of Claude Monet's outstanding "Water Lilies" paintings.

Ando erhielt den Auftrag, ein Anwesen aus den 1920er Jahren so umzugestalten und mit der nötigen Infrastruktur zu versehen, dass es als Kunstmuseum genutzt werden konnte. Obwohl das vorhandene Gebäude zu einer Zeit gebaut worden war, als in der japanischen Baukunst kaum westlicher Einfluss zu verzeichnen war, ließ sich der damalige Bauherr vom Tudorstil inspirieren, den er während seines Studiums in England kennengelernt hatte. Tadao Ando strebte nach einer stimulierender Interaktion zwischen dieser dekorativen Architektur und moderem, offenen Raum. Er errichtete neben dem Altbau einen runden Ausstellungsraum von sechs Metern Durchmesser, der teilweise im Gelände versenkt wurde, um den Blick über die ursprüngliche Anlage nicht zu beeinträchtigen. Das Dach dieses Baus wurde begrünt, ebenso wie die neuen Außenanlagen, so dass der Komplex sich homogen in seine Umgebung einfügt. Die beiden voneinander unabhängigen Gebäude sind über einen Treppengang miteinander verbunden und bieten dem Betrachter völlig unterschiedliche Raumerlebnisse. Der Altbau beherbergt die komplette Keramiksammlung, während der Neubau bedeutende Werke des Impressionismus aufnimmt, darunter auch eines von Claude Monets „Seerosen"-Bildern.

La commande avait pour objet de doter une maison des années vingt du XXème siècle des infrastructures nécessaires afin de la convertir en musée d'art. En dépit du fait que la maison existante date d'une époque où l'influence occidentale était tout juste notable dans la construction japonaise, le propriétaire s'était inspiré du style Tudor qu'il avait observé lors de ses études en Angleterre. Tadao Ando a voulu créer une interaction stimulante entre cette architecture aux détails expressifs et l'architecture moderne, avec son espace ouvert. À côté du bâtiment original fut érigée une galerie cylindrique de six mètres de diamètre, partiellement enterrée afin de ne pas faire obstacle à la perception continue l'ancienne maison et du jardin. En outre, la toiture fut couverte de végétation, ainsi que les alentours de la nouvelle construction, de sorte que l'ensemble se mêle harmonieusement avec son environnement. Les deux édifices, indépendants et autonomes, sont connectés par des escaliers et offrent des expériences spatiales très distinctes. Le plus ancien accueille une collection complète de céramiques, alors que le plus récent présente des œuvres impressionnistes notables, parmi lesquelles une des paintures de « Nymphéas » de Claude Monet.

L'incarico consisteva nel dotare una casa degli anni venti del XX° secolo delle infrastrutture necessarie per trasformarla in un museo d'arte. Nonostante l'edificio esistente fosse stato costruito in un'epoca nella quale l'influenza occidentale cominciava appena a farsi sentire nelle costruzioni giapponesi, il proprietario si era ispirato agli edifici stile Tudor osservati mentre studiava in Inghilterra. Tadao Ando ha voluto creare una interazione stimolante tra questa architettura ricca di dettagli expressivi e uno spazio moderno aperto. Accanto all'edificio originario è stata eretta una galleria cilindrica di sei metri di diametro, parzialmente interrata per non ostacolare la veduta della casa e del giardino. Sulla copertura e nei dintorni della costruzione cilindrica è stata piantata della vegetazione per assicurare un'armoniosa fusione con l'ambiente originario. I due edifici, indipendenti ed autonomi, sono collegati con delle scale ed offrono esperienze spaziali molto differenti. Il vecchio edificio accoglie una collezione completa di ceramiche, mentre il nuovo espone importanti opere dell'impressionismo, quali una delle pitture delle "Ninfee" di Monet.

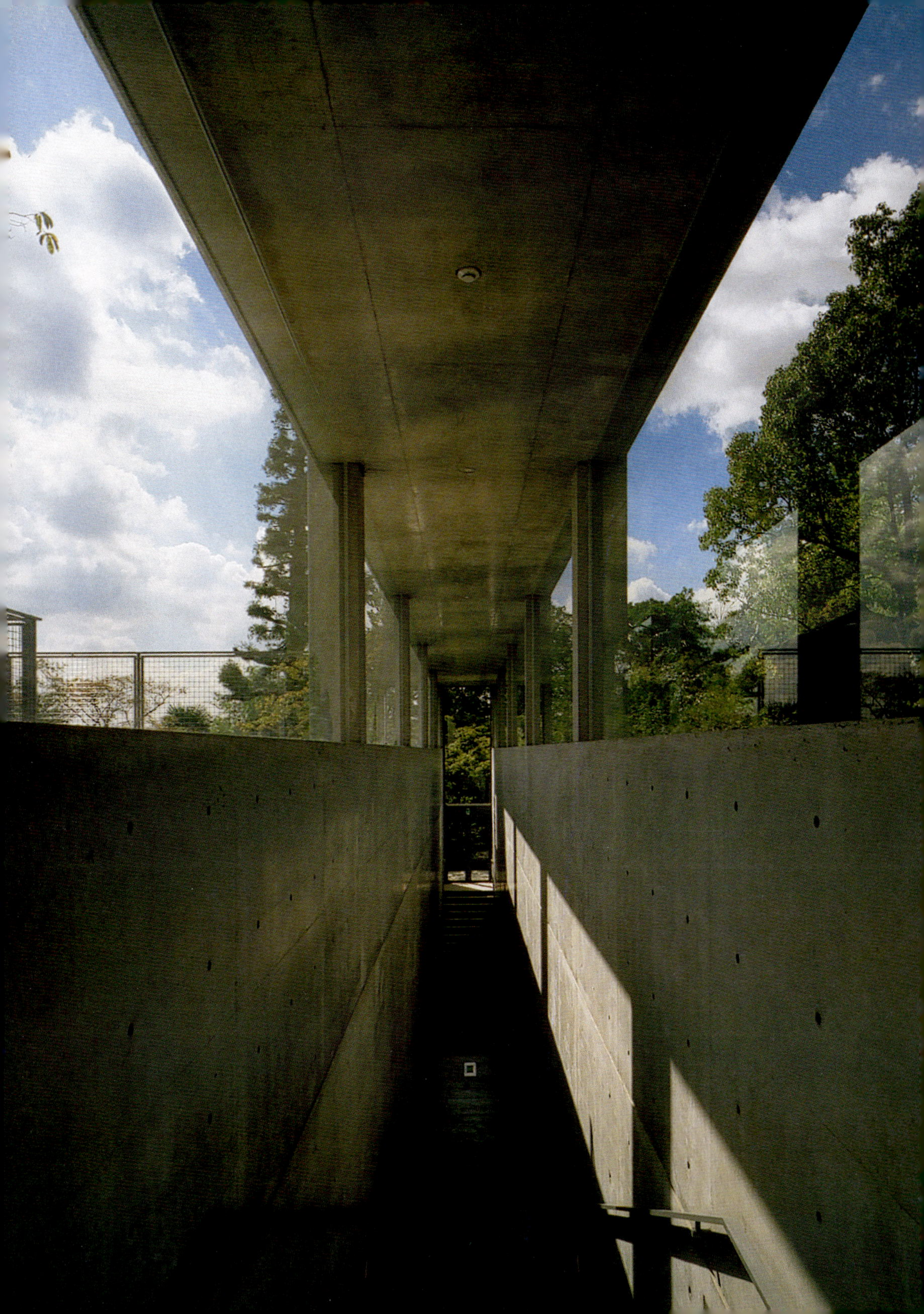

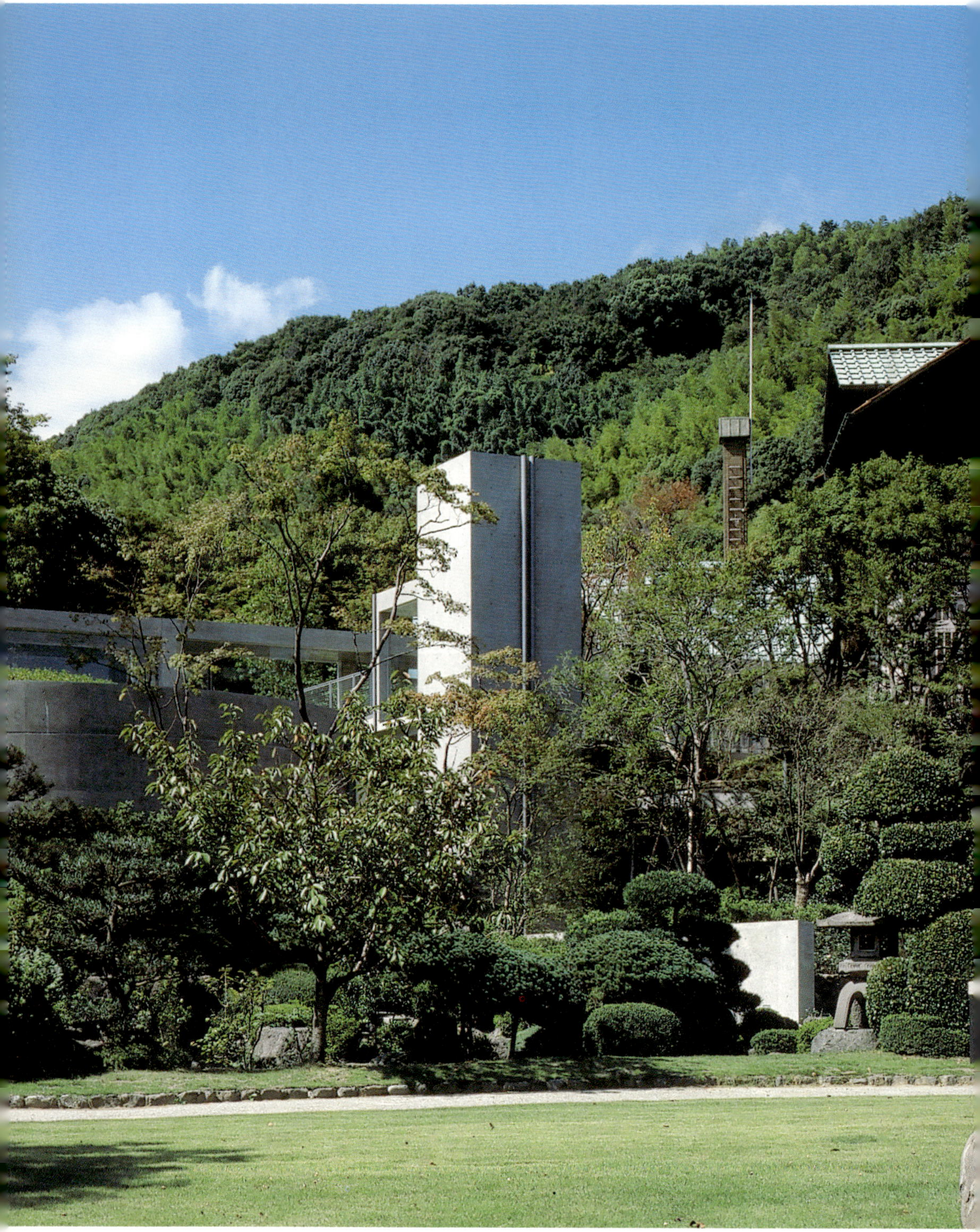

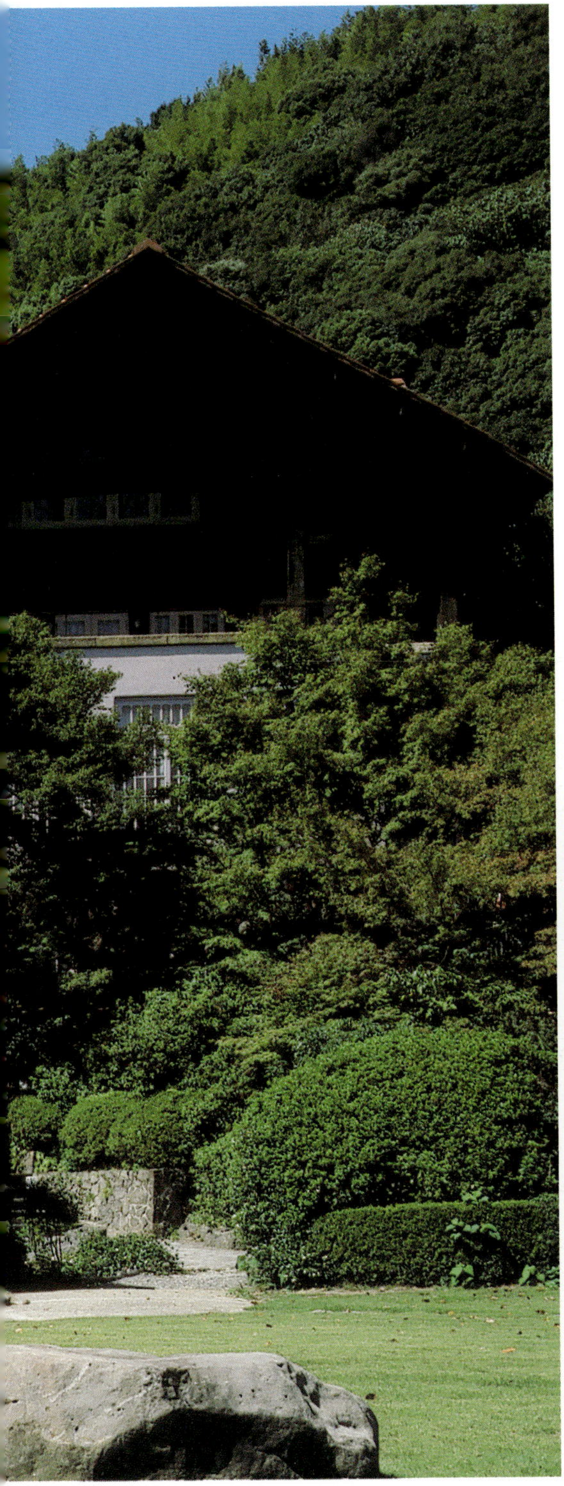

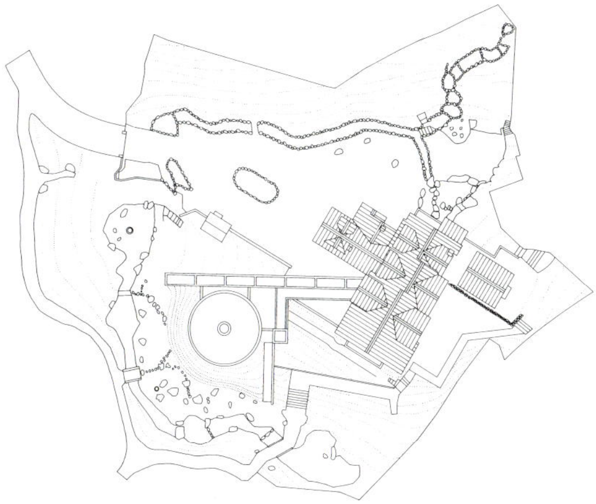

Site plan
Lageplan
Plan de situation
Pianta del sito

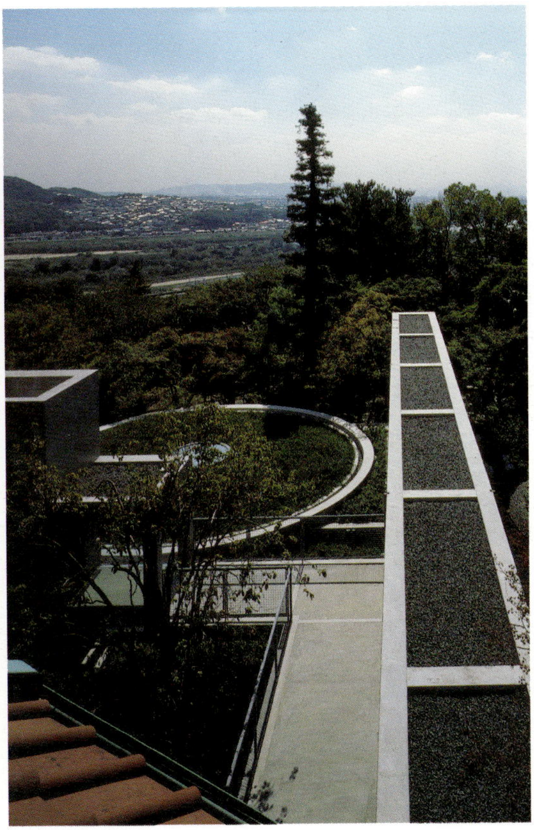

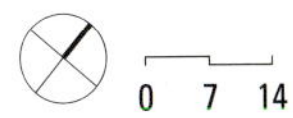

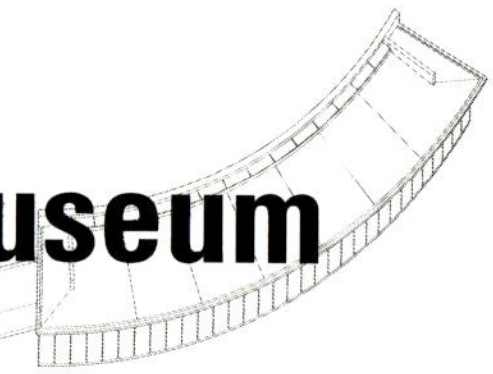

Daylight Museum

Location: Gamo, Shiga, Japan
Date of construction: 1997–1998
Photographer: Mitsuo Matsuoka

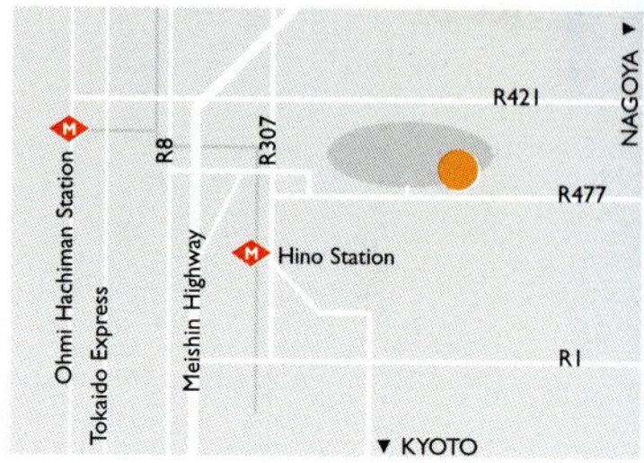

The construction of a museum dedicated to the Japanese artist Hiroki Oda greatly enthused Tadao Ando. Years before, the architect had been fascinated by a photograph of Oda that had been taken in his atelier just after the war, at a time when there was no water, no gas, no electricity. The artist had been obliged to work on his paintings only by natural light. Since then, Ando had followed the professional career of the artist in question. In contrast to today's museums, which use profuse artificial lighting to bring out the color and texture of works of art, he thought of a space that would be illumined exclusively by natural light, thus making the building harmonize with the life of the artist. The interior and the exterior of the single story building took shape from a frequently used material, concrete; the light was brought in through a system of skylights in an arched ceiling. The corridor running along the western façade receives its light through a translucent glass curtain wall. The quality and the quantity of light vary according to the time of day and the season of the year, providing many different nuances and perspectives to the visitors. Of course, the museum closes right at dusk.

Der Bau eines Museums für den japanischen Künstler Hiroki Oda erschien Tadao Ando besonders reizvoll. Der Architekt war einige Jahre zuvor von einem Foto fasziniert gewesen, das den Maler unmittelbar nach dem Krieg in seinem Atelier zeigte. Es gab kein Wasser, kein Gas und auch keinen Strom, so dass er nur bei Tageslicht an seinen Bildern arbeiten konnte. Ando verfolgte von da an die weitere Entwicklung des Künstlers. Im Gegensatz zu heutigen Museen, die in großem Umfang auf künstliches Licht zurückgreifen, um die Farben und die Oberflächenstruktur der Gemälde hervorzuheben, ersann er ein Gebäude, das nur vom Tageslicht erhellt wird und somit im Einklang mit dem Leben des Künstlers steht. Der eingeschossige Bau wurde aus Beton errichtet, das Licht fällt durch eine Reihe von Oberlichtern durch das geschwungene Dach. Der hinter der Westfassade gelegene Gang erhält sein Licht durch große Milchglasfenster. Menge und Art des einfallenden Lichts verändern sich im Laufe des Tages und entsprechend den Jahreszeiten und es bietet sich dem Besucher ein immer neues Schauspiel. Dass das Museum nur bis Sonnenuntergang geöffnet ist, versteht sich von selbst.

La construction d'un musée dédié à l'artiste japonais Hiroki Oda a enthousiasmé Tadao Ando. Des années auparavant, l'architecte était resté fasciné par une photo du peintre prise dans son atelier, juste après la guerre ; sans eau, ni gaz et sans électricité, il avait dû composer ses œuvres à la seule lumière du jour. Dès lors, Ando a suivi la trajectoire professionnelle de l'artiste. À l'inverse des musées contemporains, recourant à l'illumination artificielle à profusion afin de souligner la couleur et la texture des peintures, Ando a conçu un édifice illuminé exclusivement par la lumière naturelle. Les œuvres sont ainsi présentées à l'unisson avec la vie de l'artiste. L'intérieur et l'extérieur de l'édifice, comportant un seul étage, ont été bâtis de béton et la lumière y pénètre grâce à un système de claires-voies dans un toit arqué. Le couloir parcourant la façade ouest reçoit la lumière d'une paroi de verre translucide. La qualité et la quantité de lumière varient au cours de la journée et de l'année et proposent ainsi des visions multiples à l'observateur. Bien entendu, le musée ferme au crépuscule.

La costruzione di un museo dedicato ad l'artista giapponese Hiroki Oda stimolò profondamente Tadao Ando. Negli anni precedenti, l'architetto era rimasto affascinato da una fotografia del pittore nell suo atelier, appena dopo la guerra; non aveva acqua, gas, né elettricità, ed era obbligato a lavorare sulle proprie opere solo alla luce del giorno. Ando seguì fin da allora la carriera professionale dell'artista. In contrasto coi musei odierni che utilizzano profusamente l'illuminazione artificiale per mettere in risalto il colore e la tessitura dei quadri, decise di creare uno spazio espositivo illuminato esclusivamente dalla luce naturale, realizzando una costruzione in armonia con la vita dell'artista. L'interno e l'esterno dell'edificio – di un solo piano – sono in cemento, e la luce è introdotta mediante un sistema di lucernari inseriti nella copertura inarcata. Il corridoio che percorre la facciata ovest riceve la luce da una parete di vetro semitrasparente. La qualità e la quantità di luce cambiano durante il giorno e le stagioni dell'anno, il che fornisce all'osservatore scenari e prospettive diverse. Ovviamente il museo chiude proprio all'imbrunire.

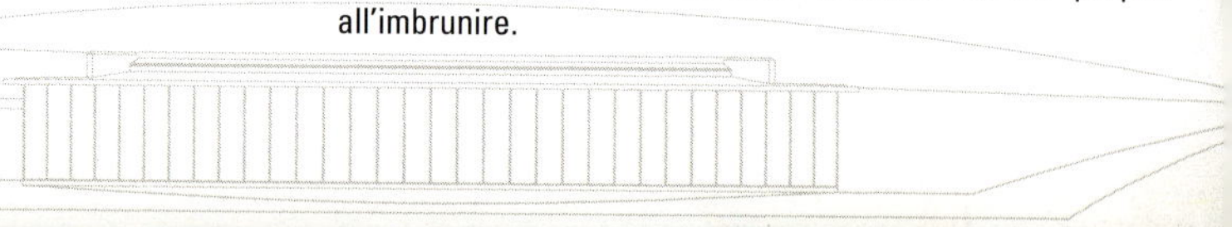

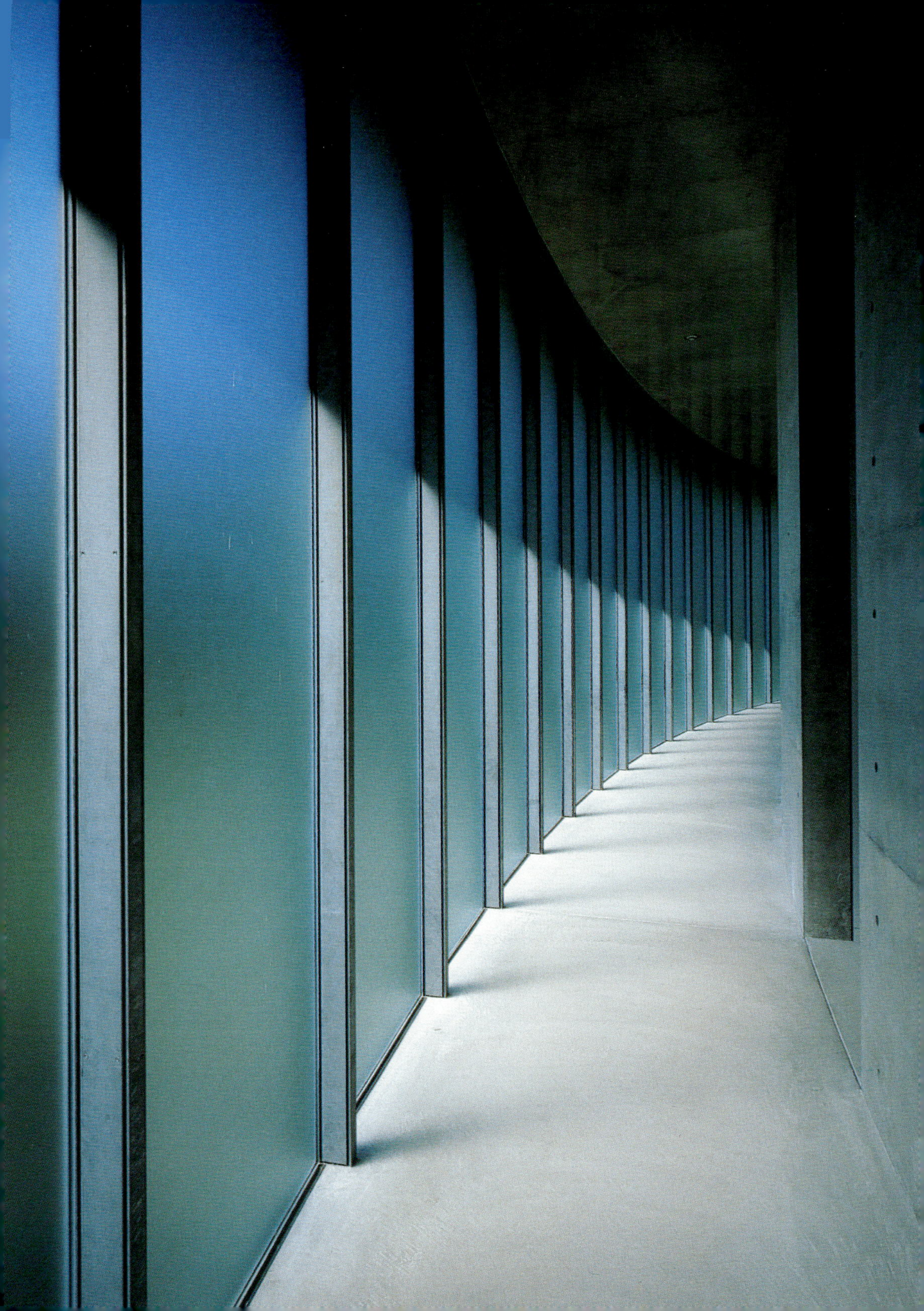

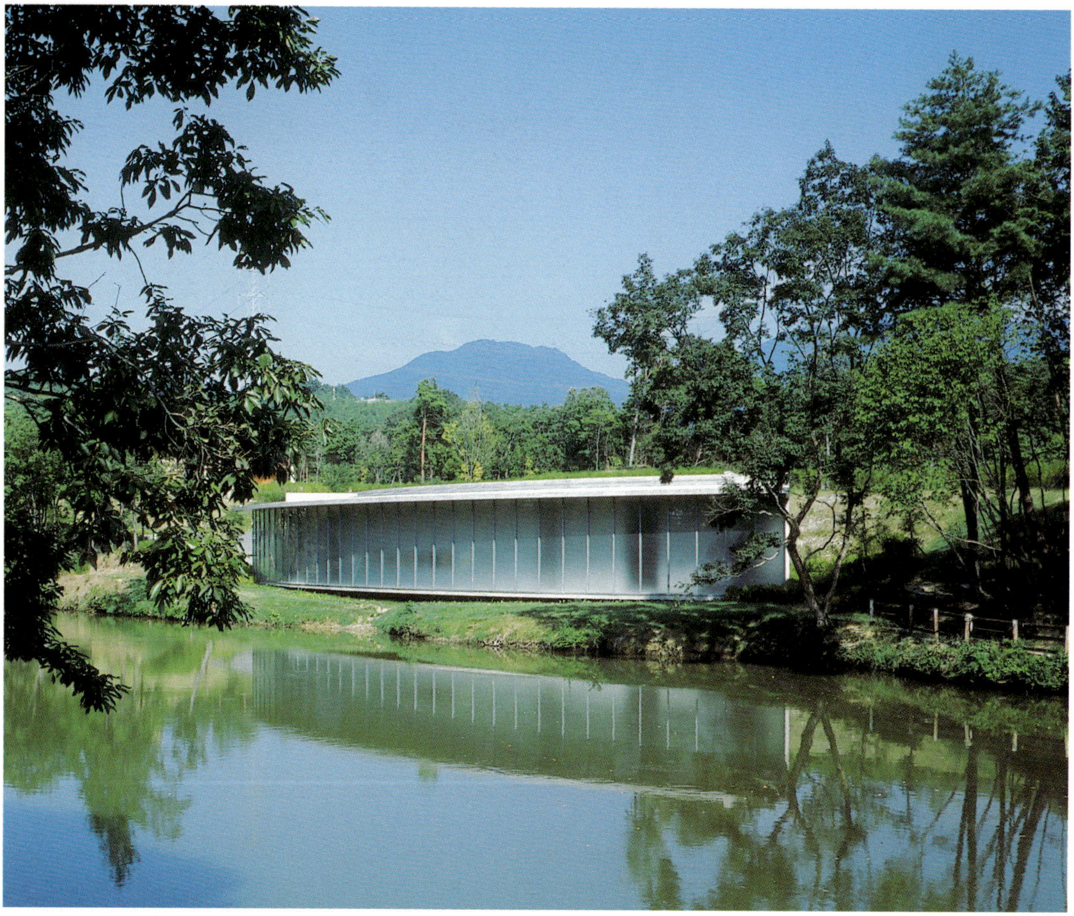

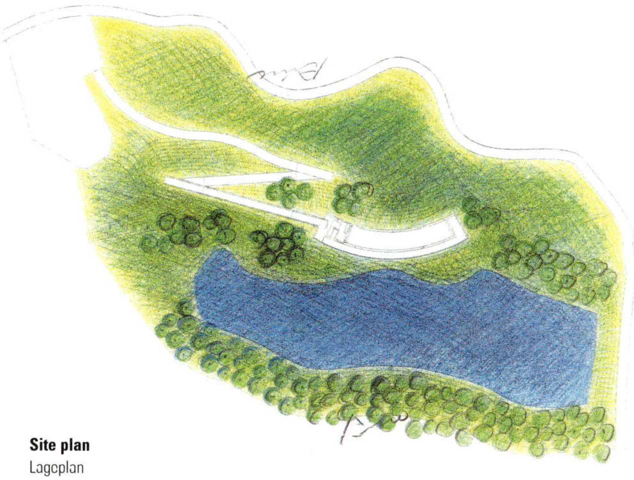

Site plan
Lageplan
Plan de situation
Pianta del sito

0 7 14

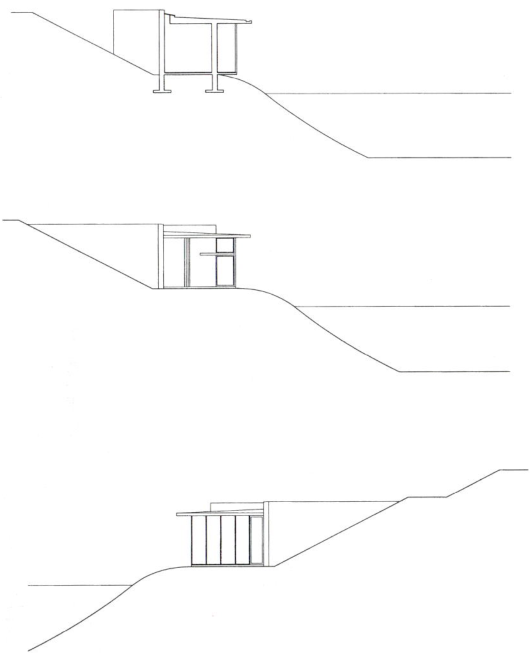

Sections
Schnitte
Sections
Sezioni

0 3 6

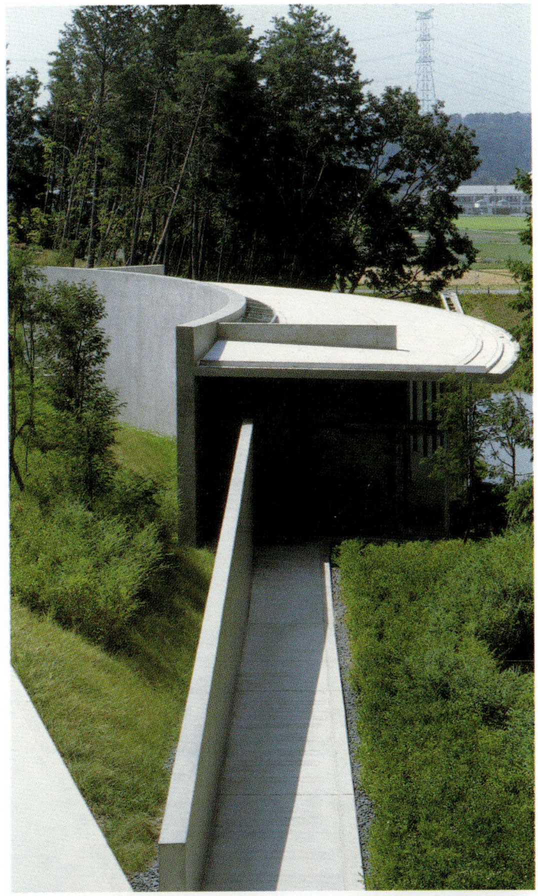

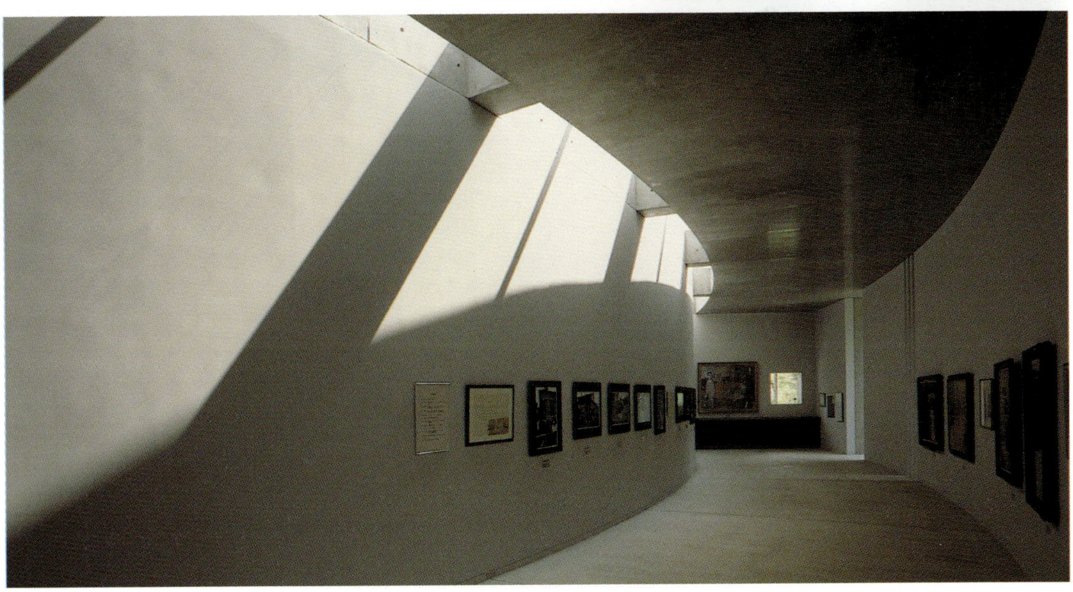

Sayamaike Historical Museum

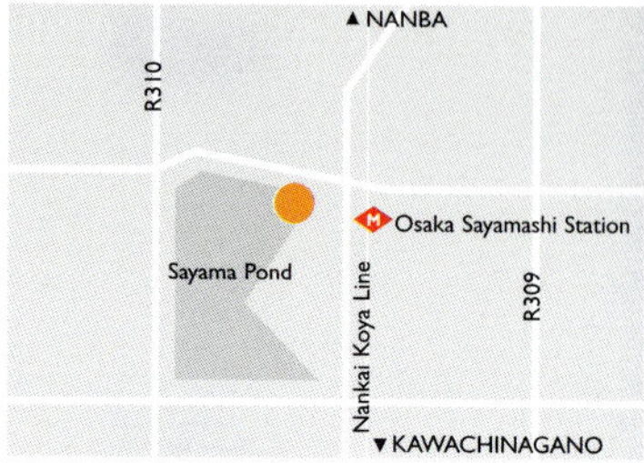

Location: Osakasayama, Osaka, Japan
Date of construction: 1997–2001
Photographers: Shigeo Ogawa, Mitsuo Matsuoka

In 1993, the restoration work on the irrigation reservoir of Sayamaike, the oldest such reservoir in Japan, in fact, uncovered the remains of some Kamakura period (1192–1333) hydraulic installations. The excavation thus brought to light the history of the repairs and improvements that had been carried out over the course of the years. Right there lay the story of Japanese civil engineering! The authorities of Osaka prefecture did not hesitate to conserve the site, and erected a museum that would put these important findings on display for the public. In order not to detract from the work being done in the field, Tadao Ando decided to design an enclosure that would make the environment itself the museum. The functional installations like service areas and offices were put on a subterranean level to keep from interfering with the continuity and serenity of the deposit. Above grade, only large-scale type walls were raised to guide the visitors. These have a monumentality that dignifies the piece. The volume of the built elements was determined by the scale of an excavated cross section of the reservoir's dam, which clearly constitute the nucleus of the exhibition.

Im Jahre 1993 wurden während Instandsetzungsarbeiten am Wasserreservoir von Sayamaike, dem ältesten in Japan, die Reste von Wasserbaueinrichtungen aus der Kamakura-Periode (1192–1333) entdeckt. Durch die Ausgrabungen konnte die historische Abfolge der verschiedenen Reparaturen und Verbesserungen rekonstruiert werden, die im Laufe der Jahrhunderte erfolgt waren. Hier liegen die Wurzeln des zivilen japanischen Ingenieurwesens, weshalb die Präfektur von Osaka beschloss, den geschichtsträchtigen Boden unter Schutz zu stellen und ein Museum einzurichten, um der Bevölkerung diese bedeutenden Funde zugänglich zu machen. Um Eingriffe vor Ort nach Möglichkeit zu vermeiden, entwarf Ando ein Projekt, bei dem der Fundort selbst zum Museum wird. Die Verwaltungs- und Diensträume wurden unterirdisch angelegt, um den Gesamteindruck des Bodenfunds nicht zu stören. Oberhalb der Erdoberfläche wurden nur einige große Mauern errichtet, die die Besucher leiten und der Anlage einen monumentalen Charakter verleihen. Die Proportionen der Neubauten orientieren sich an den Maßen eines ausgegrabenen Querschnittes des Staubeckendeiches, dem eigentlichen Gegenstand der Ausstellung.

En 1993, les travaux de restauration du réservoir d'irrigation de Sayamaike, le plus ancien du Japon, ont mis à jour les restes d'installations hydrauliques de l'ère Kamakura (1192–1333). Les fouilles ont révélé la chronique historique des réparations et des améliorations apportées au fil des siècles. Dans ce site repose l'histoire de l'ingénierie civile japonaise. De ce fait, les autorités de la préfecture d'Osaka ont décidé de préserver le lieu et d'y ériger un musée présentant au public ces découvertes d'importance. Afin de ne pas altérer les interventions du terrain, Tadao Ando a décidé de projeter un ensemble où l'environnement se convertirait lui-même en un musée. Les installations fonctionnelles, ainsi les espaces de service et bureaux, ont été situées dans des niveaux souterrains afin de ne pas interférer avec la continuité et la sérénité du site. Au dessus de la cote zéro, seuls ont été érigés des murs de grandes dimensions guidant le visiteur et conférant sa dignité à l'ensemble de par leur monumentalité. Le volume des éléments construits a été determiné par l'échelle d'une section de la digue, excavée et constituant le noyau de l'exposition.

Nel 1993, durante i lavori di restauro del bacino d'irrigazione Sayamaike, il più antico del Giappone, sono stati rinvenuti i resti di un impianto idraulico del periodo Kamakura (1192–1333). Gli scavi hanno rivelato la cronaca storica delle riparazioni e dei progressi che erano stati compiuti nel corso degli anni. Nell'area giaceva la storia dell'ingegneria civile giapponese, motivo per cui le autorità della regione di Osaka decisero di salvaguardare il luogo ed erigere un museo che facesse conoscere alla popolazione quegli importanti ritrovamenti. Per non snaturare gli interventi sul terreno, Tadao Ando decise di progettare un complesso che convertisse l'ambiente stesso in un museo. Gli impianti funzionali, come servizi ed uffici, furono collocati nei sotterranei per non interferire con la continuità e la serenità della zona archeologica. Al di sopra del terreno furono eretti solo dei muri di grandi dimensioni che danno dignità alla zona grazie alla loro monumentalità. Il volume degli elementi costruiti è stato determinato in base alle dimensioni della sezione escavata della diga, che costituiscono il nucleo dell'esposizione.

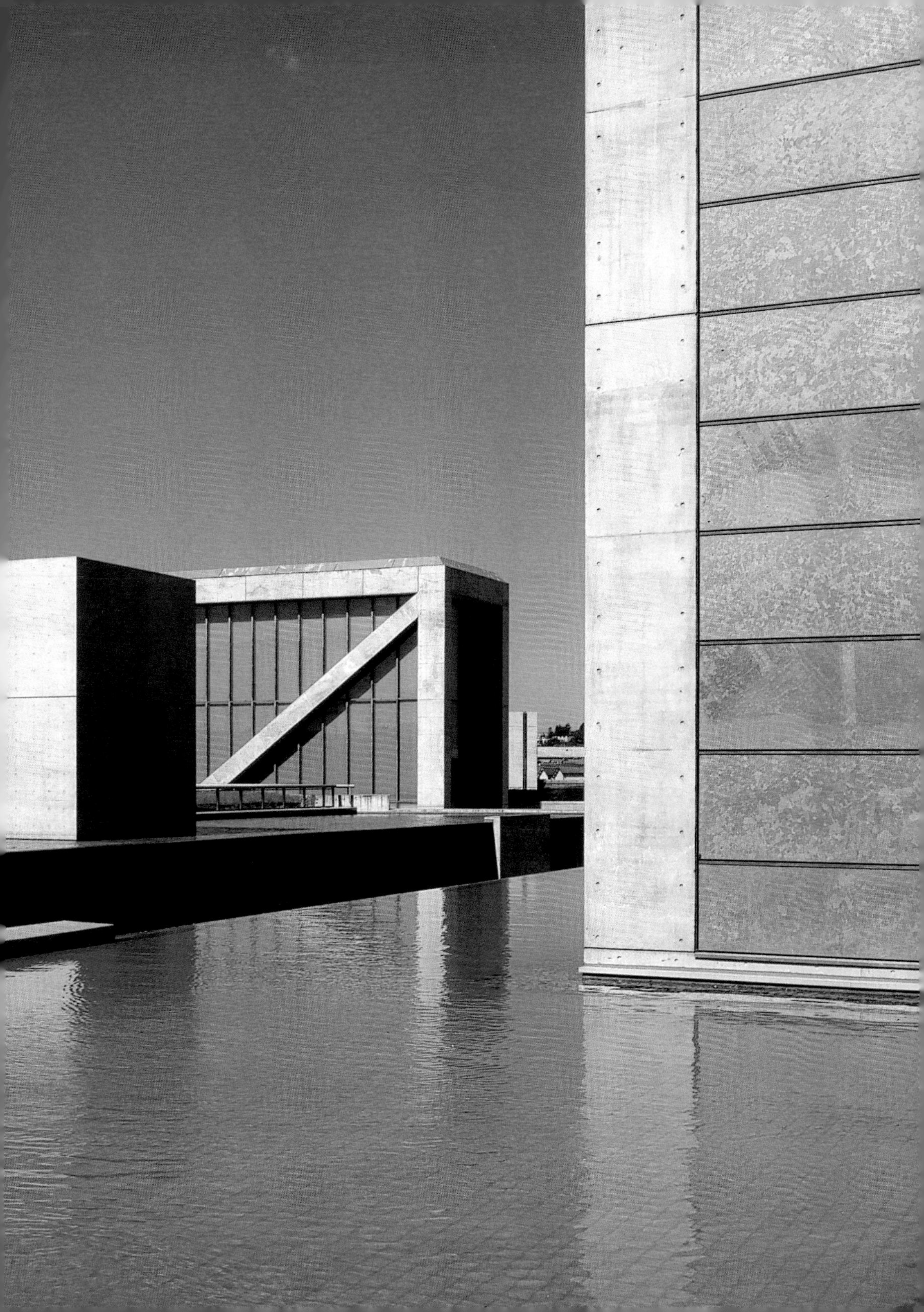

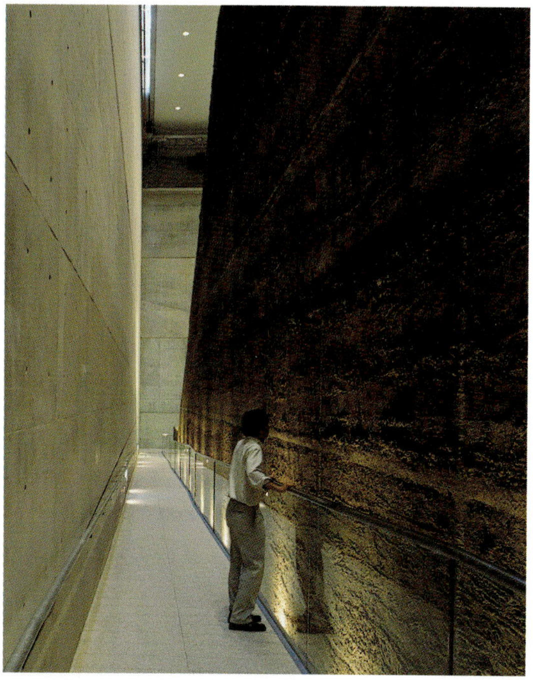

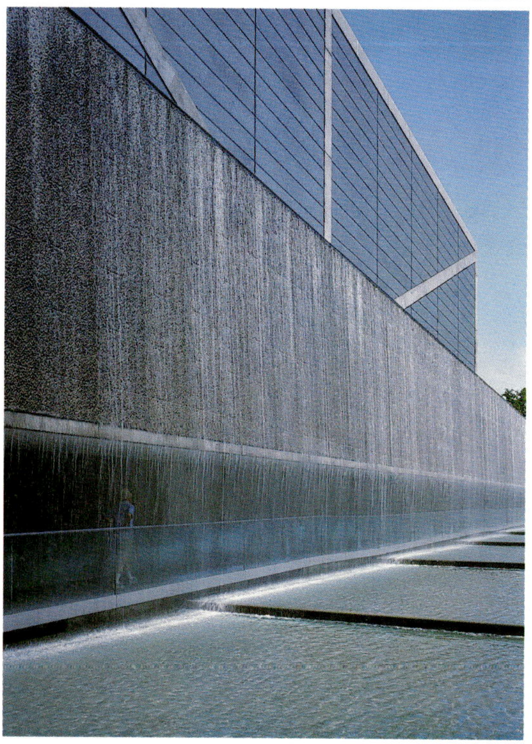

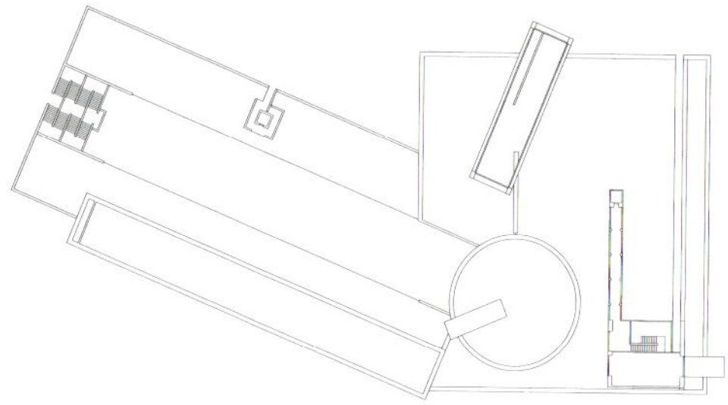

First floor
Erstes Obergeschoss
Premier étage
Piano primo

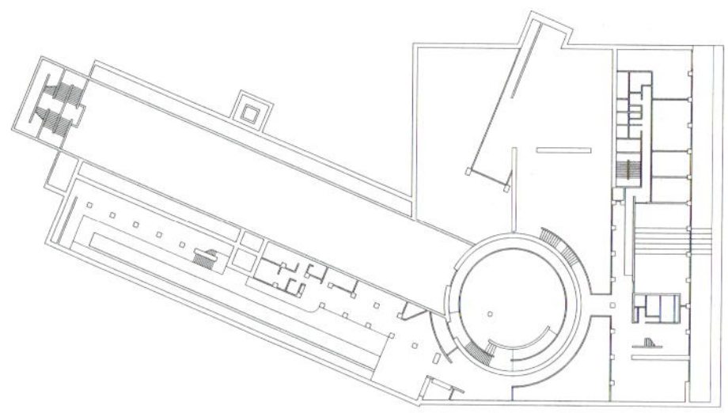

Ground floor
Erdgeschoss
Rez-de-chaussée
Piano terra

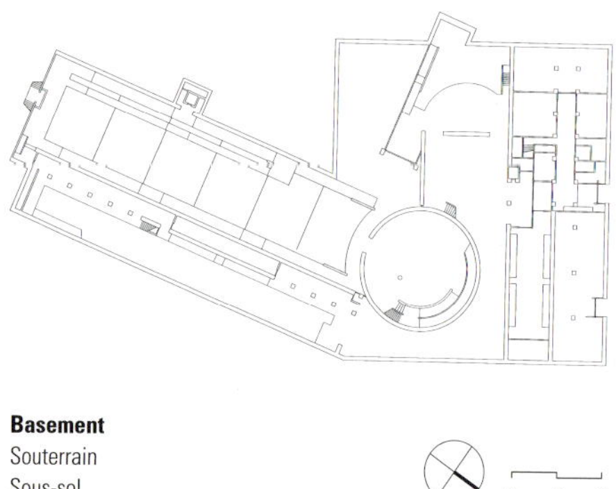

Basement
Souterrain
Sous-sol
Piano interrato

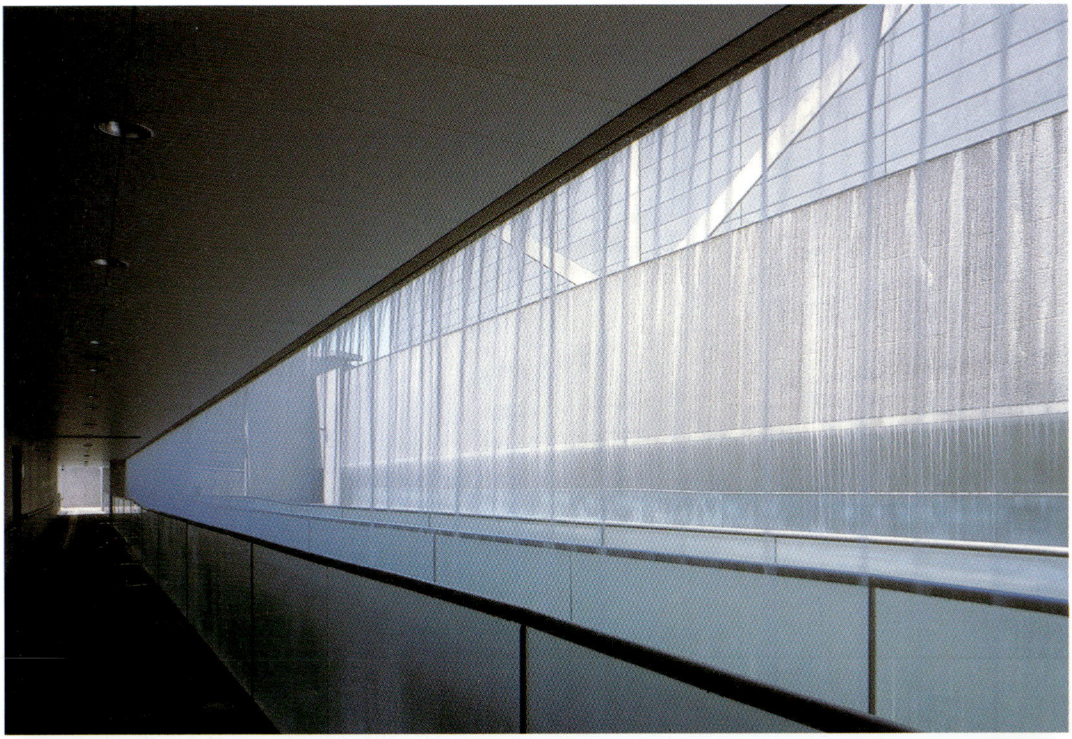

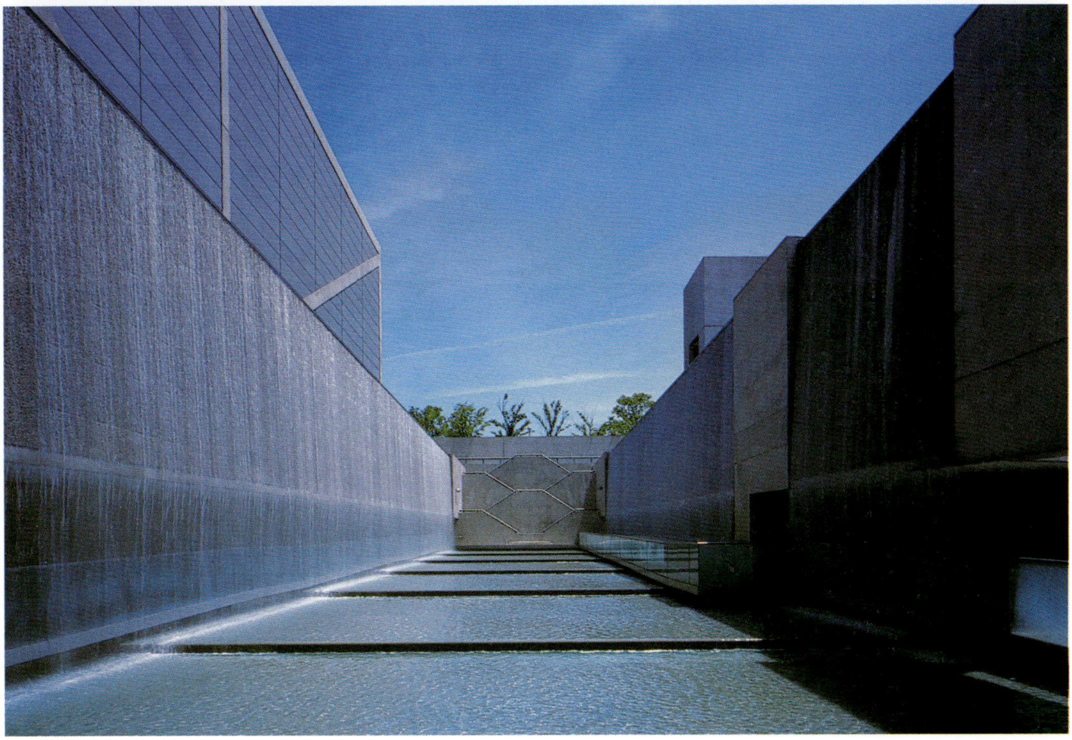

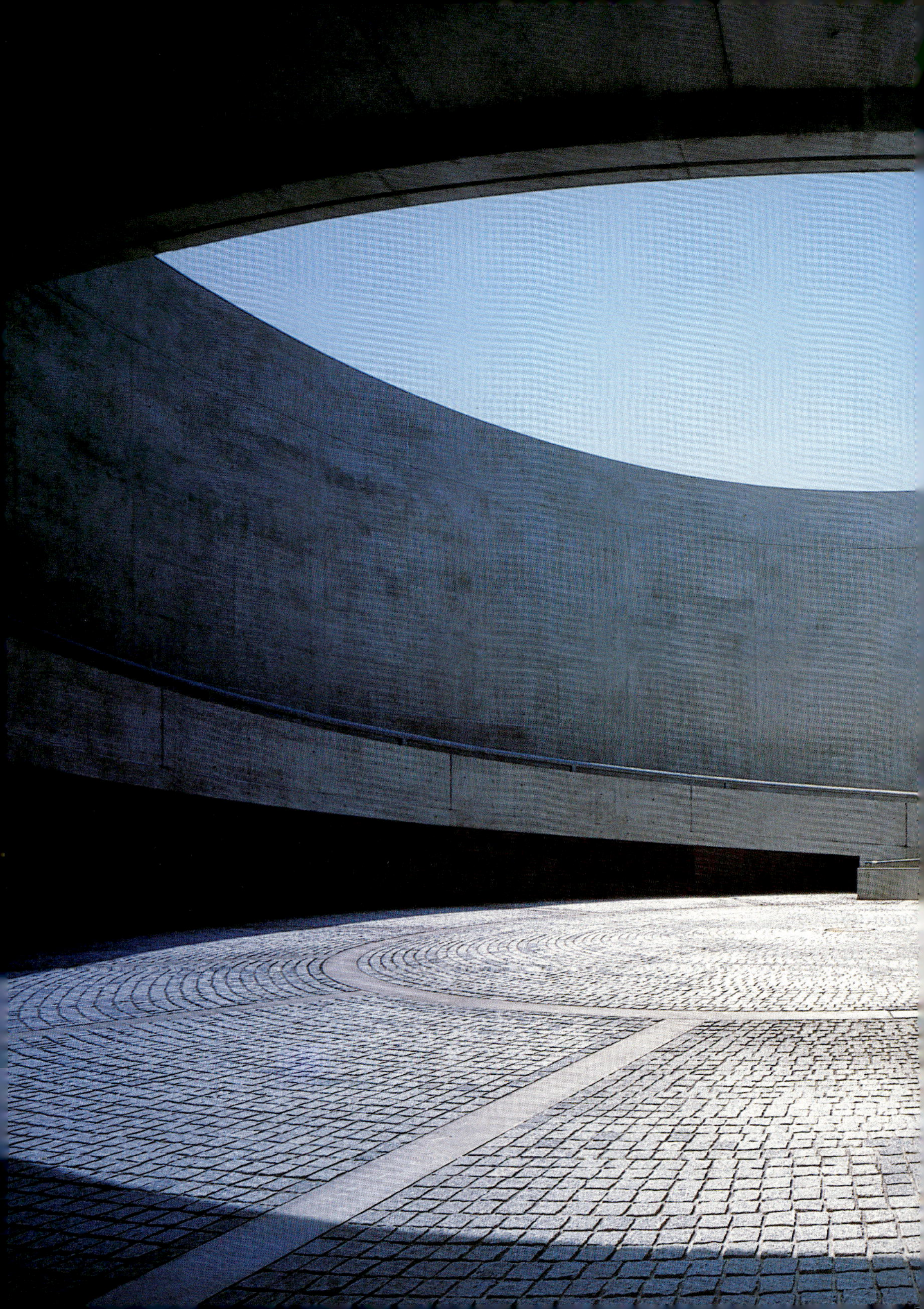

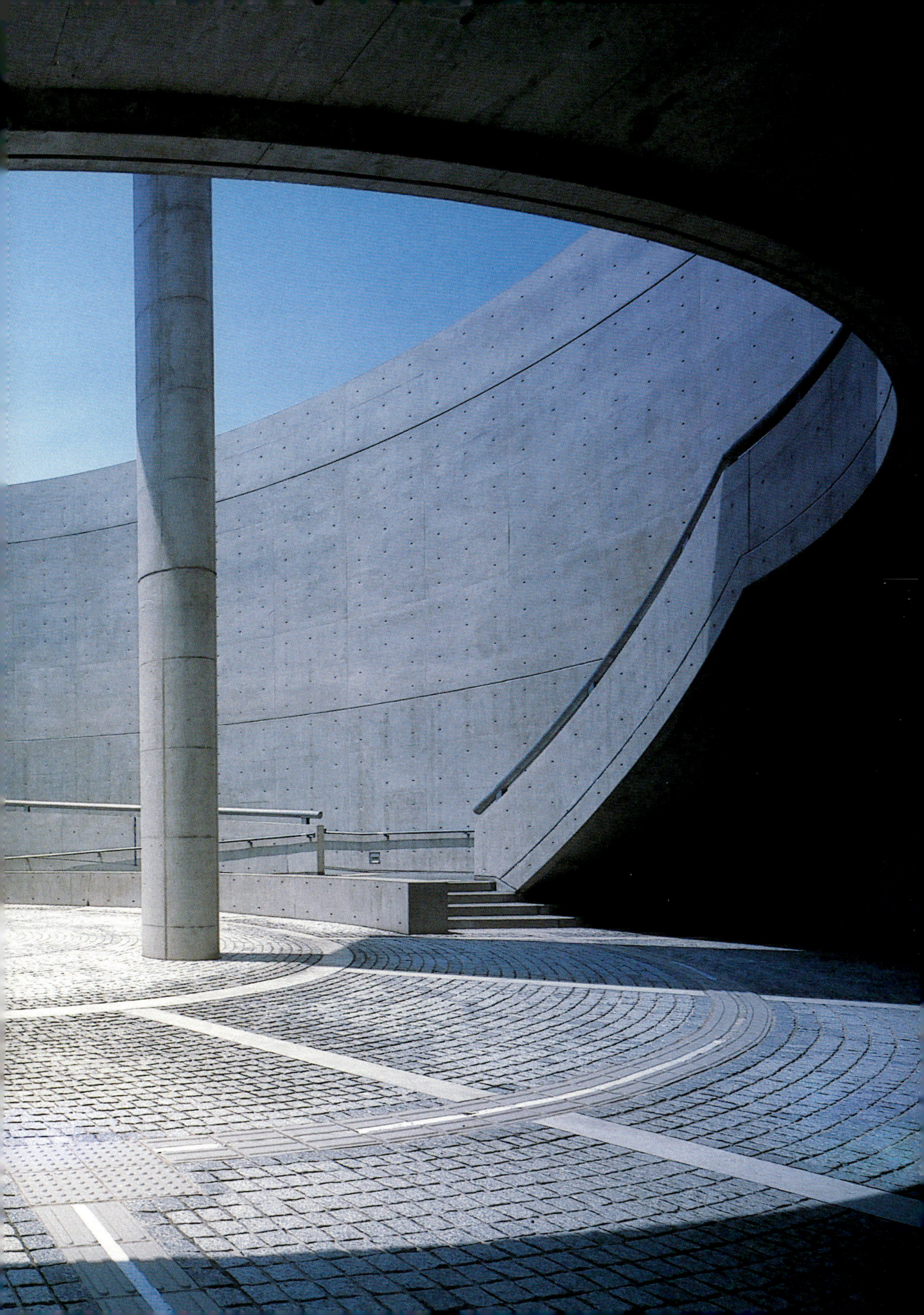

Pulitzer Foundation for the Arts

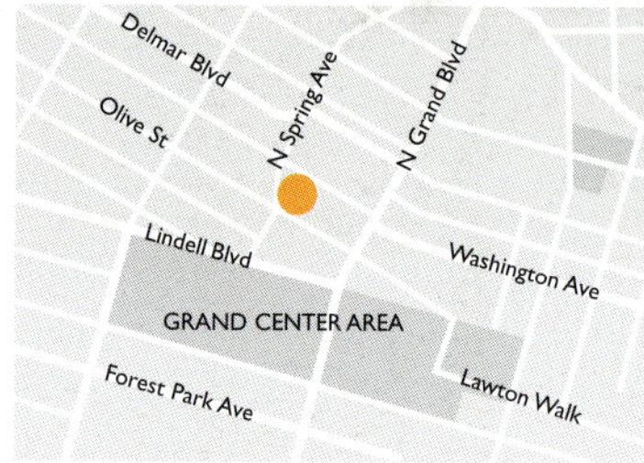

Location: Saint Louis, Missouri, USA
Date of construction: 1997–2001
Photographer: Makoto Yamamori

This new museum is to house the art collection of the Pulitzer family. The building, set in the city of Saint Louis, is on a site located in the outskirts of a flourishing cultural district that is currently being developed to give new life to a depressed city neighborhood. Basing the work on the requirements of the clients and the specific nature of the plot of land in question, the building was given residential scale and the necessary installations for a gallery of contemporary art. The Pulitzer Foundation for the Arts is comprised of two rectangular boxes of different heights: the taller of the two volumes houses the exhibition gallery; the other, with gardened roof, has the entrance, the offices, and the library. Outside again, spaces like the water-patio that forms at the juncture of the two rectangles and the terraces link directly to the inside. It is a relationship that is played up by the apertures in the different façades. From the beginning, some of the collection's artists, like Ellsworth Kelly and Richard Serra, participated in the design. Some of the proposals may have put obstacles in the path of the project's development, but they came with an enriching perspective that benefited the final result.

Ce nouveau musée devait héberger la collection artistique de la famille Pulitzer. L'édifice, situé dans la ville de Saint Louis, occupe un terrain sur la périphérie d'un district culturel florissant, développé pour régénérer un quartier désaffecté et dégradé. En se fondant sur les impératifs fixés par les clients et la spécificité de la parcelle, une construction à échelle résidentielle à pu être bâtie pour accueillir toutes les installations propres d'une galerie d'art contemporain. Le projet comporte deux volumes rectangulaires de hauteurs distinctes. Le plus élevé abrite les salles d'expositions ; l'autre, doté d'une toiture végétalisée, comprend l'entrée, les bureaux et la bibliothèque. Les espaces extérieurs, ainsi le patio-fontaine né entre les deux volumes et les terrasses, permettent la connexion directe entre l'intérieur et l'extérieur. Cette relation se voit rehaussée par les ouvertures dans les différentes façades. Dès le départ, certains artistes de la collection, ainsi Ellsworth Kelly et Richard Serra, ont été impliqués dans la conception. Bien que certaines de leurs propositions aient pu créer des obstacles au développement du projet, ils ont cependant apporté une vision enrichissante dont le résultat final a amplement bénéficié.

Dieses neue Museum sollte die Kunstsammlung der Familie Pulitzer aufnehmen. Es wurde im Rahmen der Stadterneuerung als Teil eines neuerdings florierenden Kulturviertels in einem vernachlässigten Stadtteil von Saint Louis errichtet. Entsprechend den Wünschen des Bauherrn und den Eigenheiten des Geländes wurde ein Komplex mit allen für eine Galerie zeitgenössischer Kunst erforderlichen Einrichtungen geplant, das dennoch einen Wohnmaßstab vorweist. Der Entwurf umfasst zwei rechteckige Baukörper unterschiedlicher Höhe. Der Höhere nimmt die Ausstellungsräume auf, der Niedrigere mit seinem begrünten Dach den Eingangsbereich, die Büros und die Bibliothek. Im Außenbereich – im Innenhof und Wasserbecken zwischen den beiden Gebäudeteilen sowie durch die Terrassen – wird die direkte Verbindung zwischen innen und außen unterstrichen, ebenso wie durch die Öffnungen in den Fassaden. Von Anfang an waren Künstler wie Ellsworth Kelly oder Richard Serra, die auch in der Sammlung vertreten sind, an der Entwurfsplanung beteiligt. Und obwohl einige ihrer Vorschläge die Entwicklung des Projektes eher behinderten, wirkte sich ihre Mitarbeit bereichernd auf das Endergebnis aus.

Questo nuovo museo sorge per ospitare la collezione d'arte della famiglia Pulitzer. L'edificio, situato nella città di Saint Louis, occupa uno spazio alla periferia di un fiorente distretto culturale che si sta sviluppando per rigenerare un quartiere urbanisticamente degradato. Basandosi sulle richieste dei clienti e sulle particolarità del lotto, è stato costruito un edificio a scala residenziale che contiene tutte le installazioni proprie di una galleria d'arte contemporanea. La fondazione si compone di due volumi rettangolari di diversa altezza; il più alto accoglie le sale d'esposizione, e l'altro, che ha una copertura a giardino, ospita l'entrata, gli uffici e la biblioteca. Gli spazi esterni, come il cortile-fontana collocato all'incrocio dei due volumi rettangolari e le terrazze, permettono il collegamento diretto dell'interno con gli spazi all'aria aperta, relazione che viene enfatizzata dalle aperture sulle varie facciate. Fin dal principio, alcuni degli artisti della collezione, come Ellsworth Kelly e Richard Serra, hanno partecipato alla progettazione. Nonostante alcune delle loro proposte abbiano ostacolato lo sviluppo del progetto, hanno però apportato una visione arricchita che ha beneficiato il risultato finale.

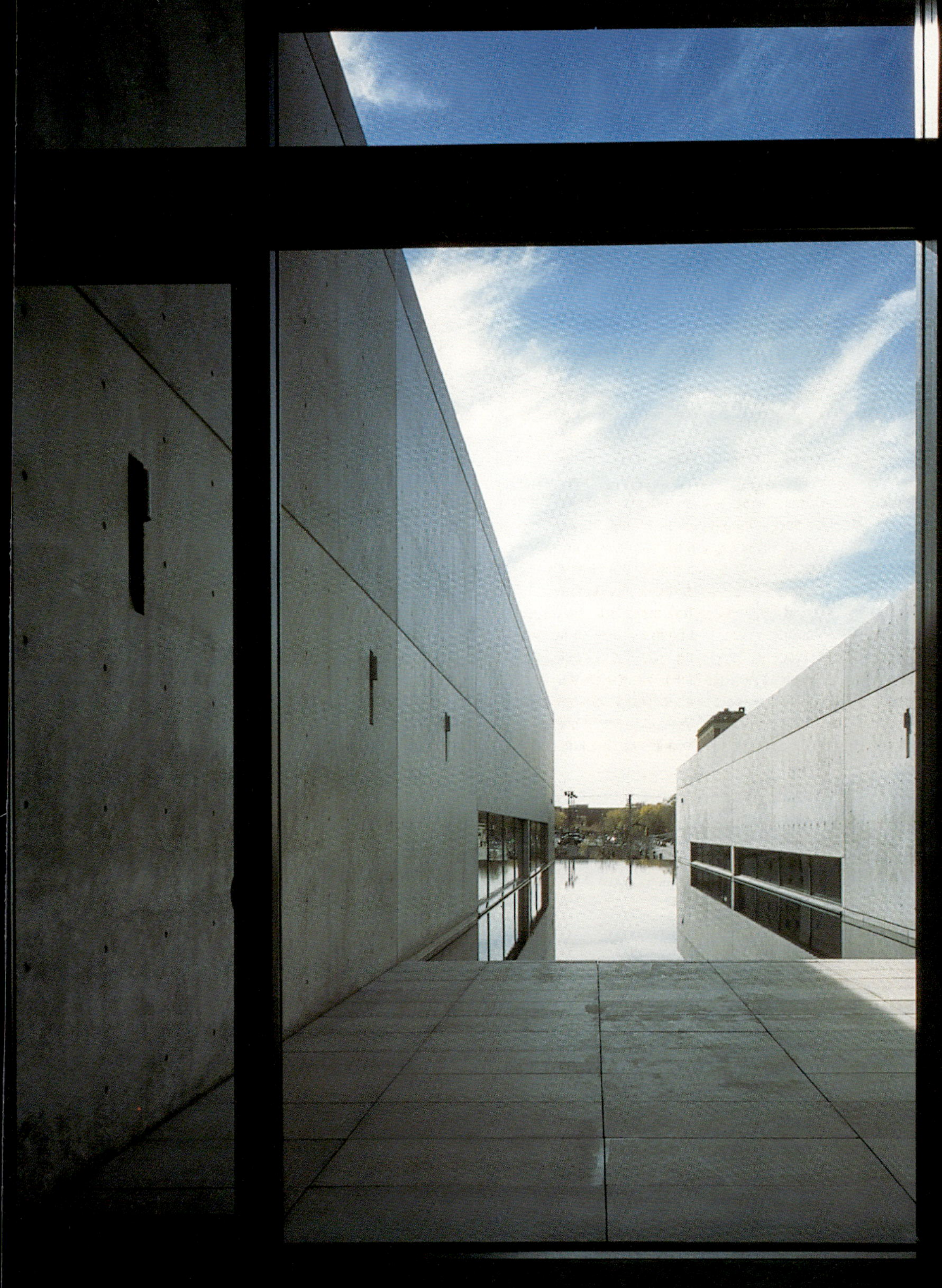

First floor Erstes Obergeschoss
Premier étage **Piano primo**

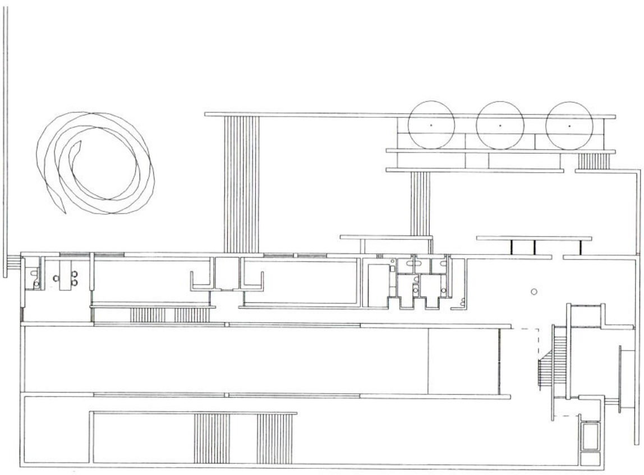

Ground floor Erdgeschoss
Rez-de-chaussée **Piano terra**

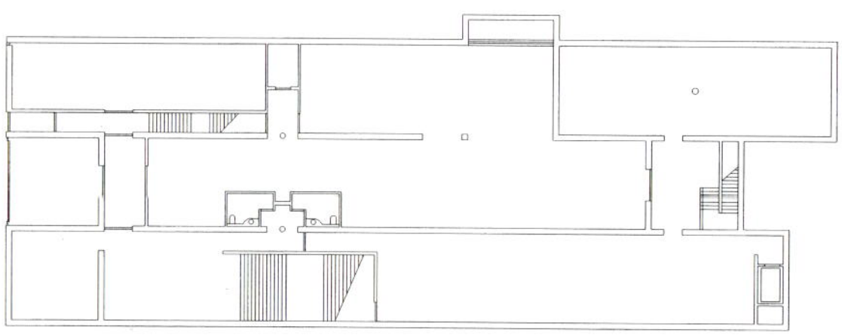

Basement Souterrain
Sous-sol **Piano interrato**

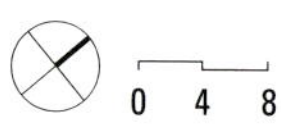

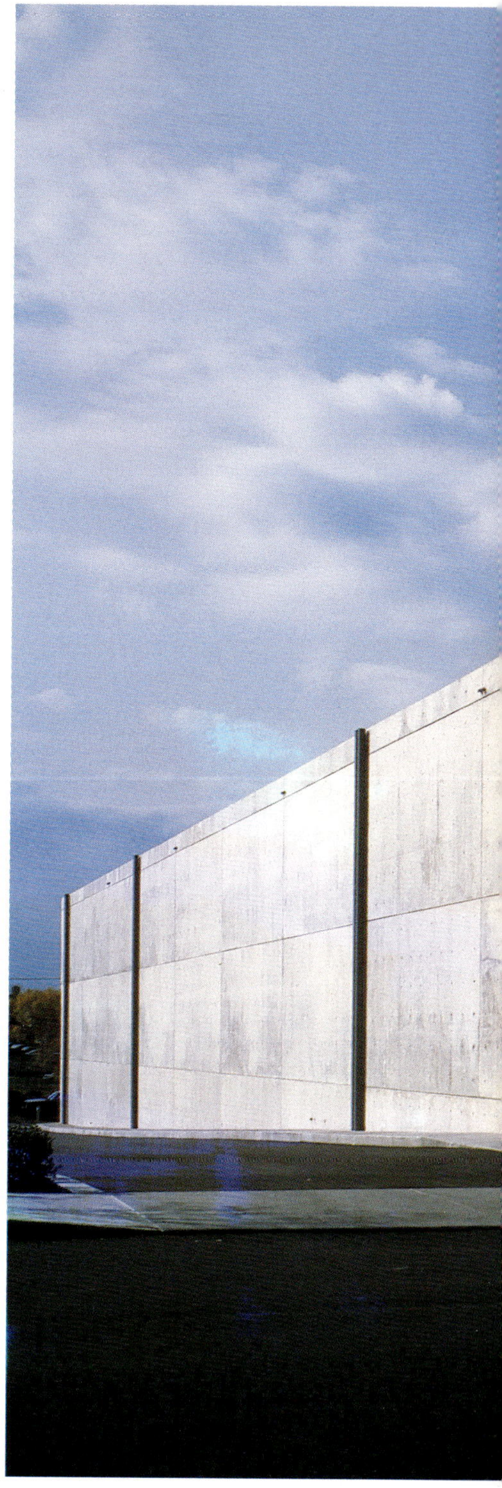

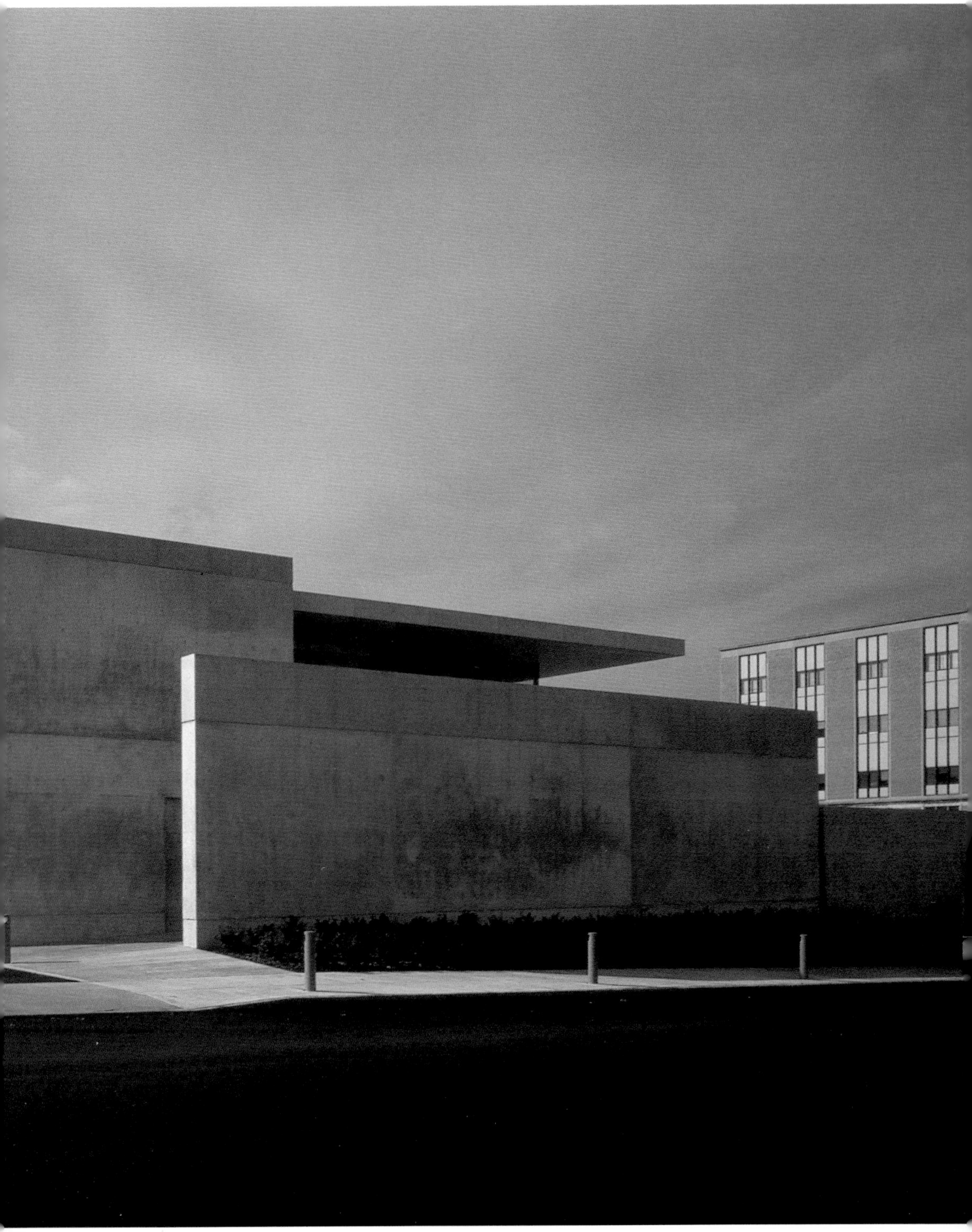

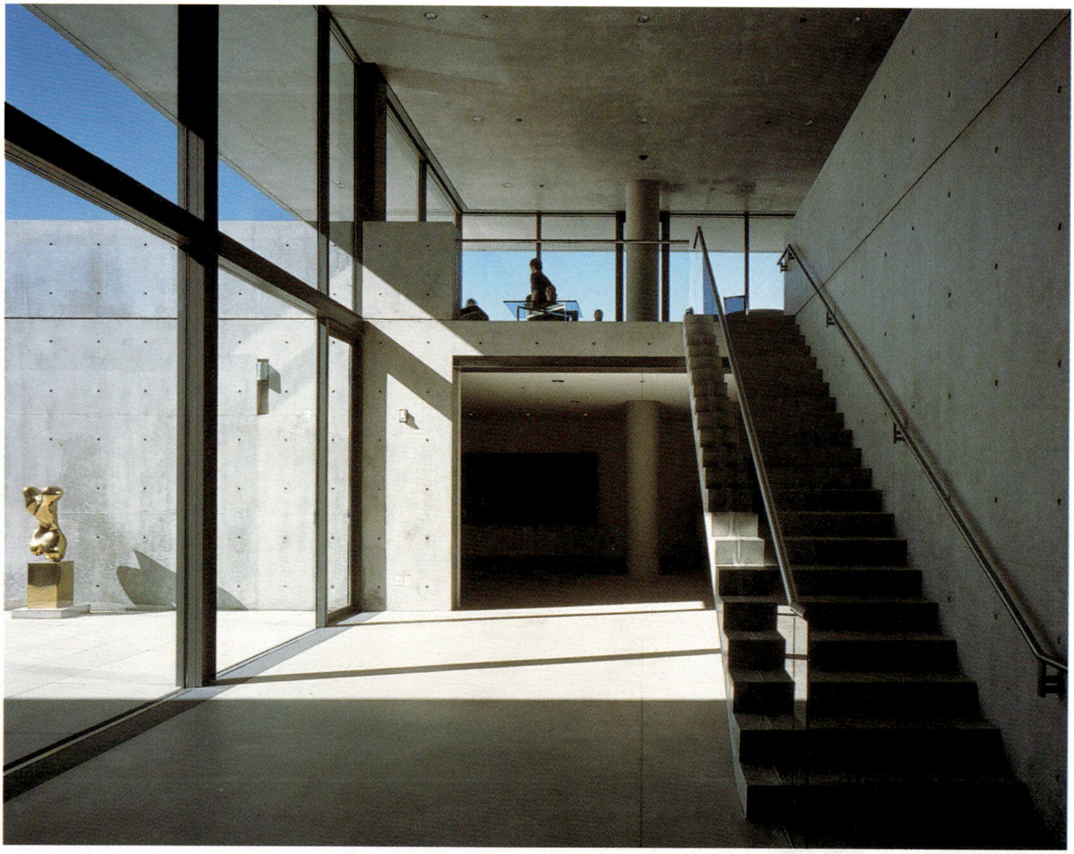

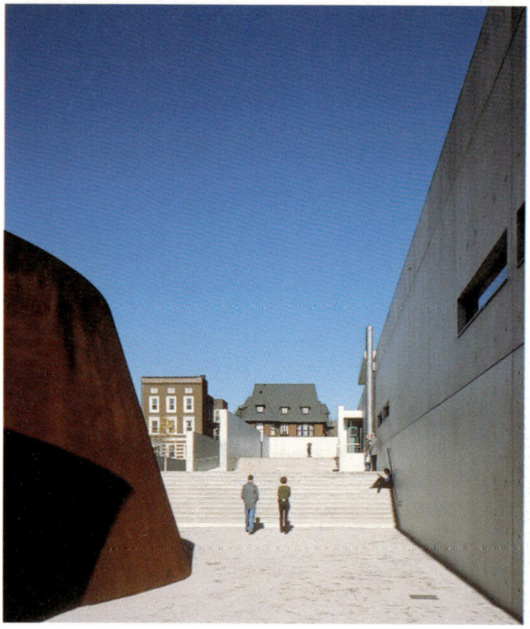

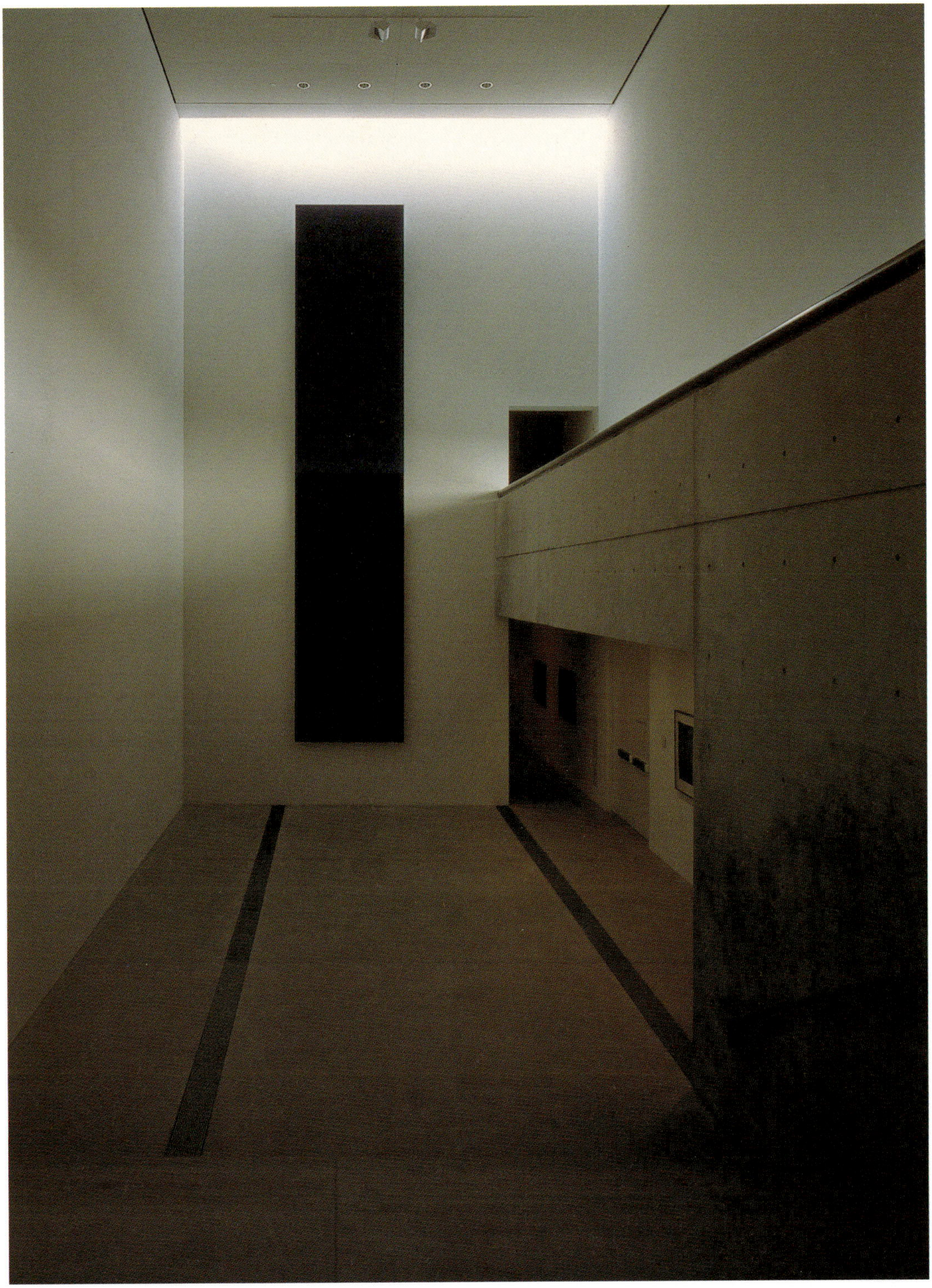

Hyogo Prefectural Museum of Art – Kobe Waterfront Plaza

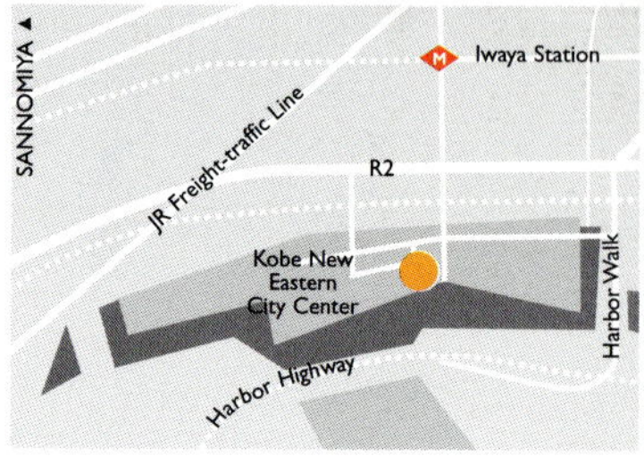

Location: Kobe, Hyogo, Japan
Date of construction: 1998–2001
Photographer: Mitsuo Matsuoka

After the dramatic earthquake that took place in 1995, the authorities of Hyogo prefecture and those of the city of Kobe proposed the reconstruction of the oceanfront of the city as a symbol of the physical and moral recovery of the community. This symbol is located to the east of the city, at one end of the harbor where, earlier, important iron and steel industries standed. Tadao Ando was chosen to design two of the most noteworthy structures for the new neighborhood: a large municipal park on the ocean shore and the museum of fine art of the prefecture of Hyogo. While the fact that there were two clients did little to facilitate the articulation between the two proposals, it at least generated a negotiating challenge for the architectural office. The museum combines stone walls and three glass enclosed volumes that receive the art display rooms. A passageway serves as functional interface between museum and park, the latter designed as refuge area in case of another earthquake. Its central zone can double as the scene of recreational-cultural activities. Camphor trees, the official tree of this prefecture, were planted and sculptures were placed.

Nach dem verheerenden Erdbeben von 1995 beschlossen die Behörden der Präfektur Hyogo gemeinsam mit den Stadtvätern von Kobe, dass der Wiederaufbau der Küstenlinie ein Symbol des physischen und moralischen Neubeginns für die Stadtgemeinschaft werden sollte. Der Planungsbereich liegt im Osten der Stadt, am Ende des Hafens, dort wo sich früher ein Eisenhüttenwerk befand. Tadao Ando erhielt den Auftrag für die beiden wichtigsten Bauvorhaben des neuen Stadtteils: ein großer Park direkt am Meer und das Kunstmuseum der Präfektur von Hyogo. Die Tatsache, dass es zwei Bauherren gab, erschwerte eine einheitliche Planung beider Projekte und stellte große Anforderungen an das Büro. Das Museum setzt sich aus Steinmauern und drei gläsernen Baukörpern zusammen, in denen die Ausstellungsräume untergebracht sind. Über eine Promenade ist das Gebäude mit dem Park verbunden, der im Falle eines weiteren Erdbebens als Zufluchtsort dient. Sein zentraler Bereich ist kulturellen Veranstaltungen vorbehalten. Es wurde vorgesehen, dass in den Außenanlagen Skulpturen aufgestellt und Kampferbäume angepflanzt werden, die Wappenbäume der Stadt.

Après le terrible tremblement de terre de 1995, les autorités de la préfecture de Hyogo en association avec celles de la ville de Kobe ont proposé la reconstruction du front de mer de la cité en symbole du rétablissement physique et moral de la communauté. Le projet a été situé à l'est de la ville, à une extrémité du port où, il y a quelques années, se dressait une importante industrie sidérurgique. Tadao Ando a été choisi pour projeter deux des interventions les plus significatives du nouveau quartier : un grand parc municipal en bord de mer et le musée d'art de la préfecture de Hyogo. En dépit du fait que l'existence de deux clients n'ait pas facilité l'unification des deux propositions, elle a néanmoins supposé un défi de négociation pour le cabinet. Le musée est composé de murs de pierre et de trois volumes vitrés accueillant les salles d'exposition. Une promenade connecte les installations avec le parc, conçu pour servir de refuge dans l'éventualité d'un autre tremblement de terre. Sa zone centrale sert de scène pour diverses activités de loisirs et culturelles. Ont été prévus, tout autour, des camphriers, l'arbre officiel de la préfecture, ainsi que des sculptures.

Dopo il drammatico terremoto del 1995, gli amministratori della prefettura di Hyogo insieme a quelli della città di Kobe proposero la ricostruzione del fronte marittimo della città come simbolo del recupero fisico e morale della comunità. L'intervento fu situato ad est della località, al margine del porto, dove anni prima esisteva un'importante industria siderurgica. Tadao Ando fu selezionato per progettare due degli interventi più significativi del nuovo quartiere: un grande parco municipale in riva al mare ed il museo d'arte della prefettura di Hyogo. Il fatto che i clienti fossero due non facilitò l'unificazione delle proposte e rappresentò per lo studio una sfida fatta di continue trattative. Il museo è costituito da muri di pietra e da tre volumi in vetro che accolgono le sale d'esposizione. Un passaggio collega gli spazi del museo al parco ed è destinato ad area di rifugio nel caso di un nuovo terremoto. La sua zona centrale può essere utilizzata anche come scenario per attività ludico-culturali. Attorno sono stati piantati degli alberi di canfora, l'albero ufficiale della regione, e sono state disposte varie sculture.

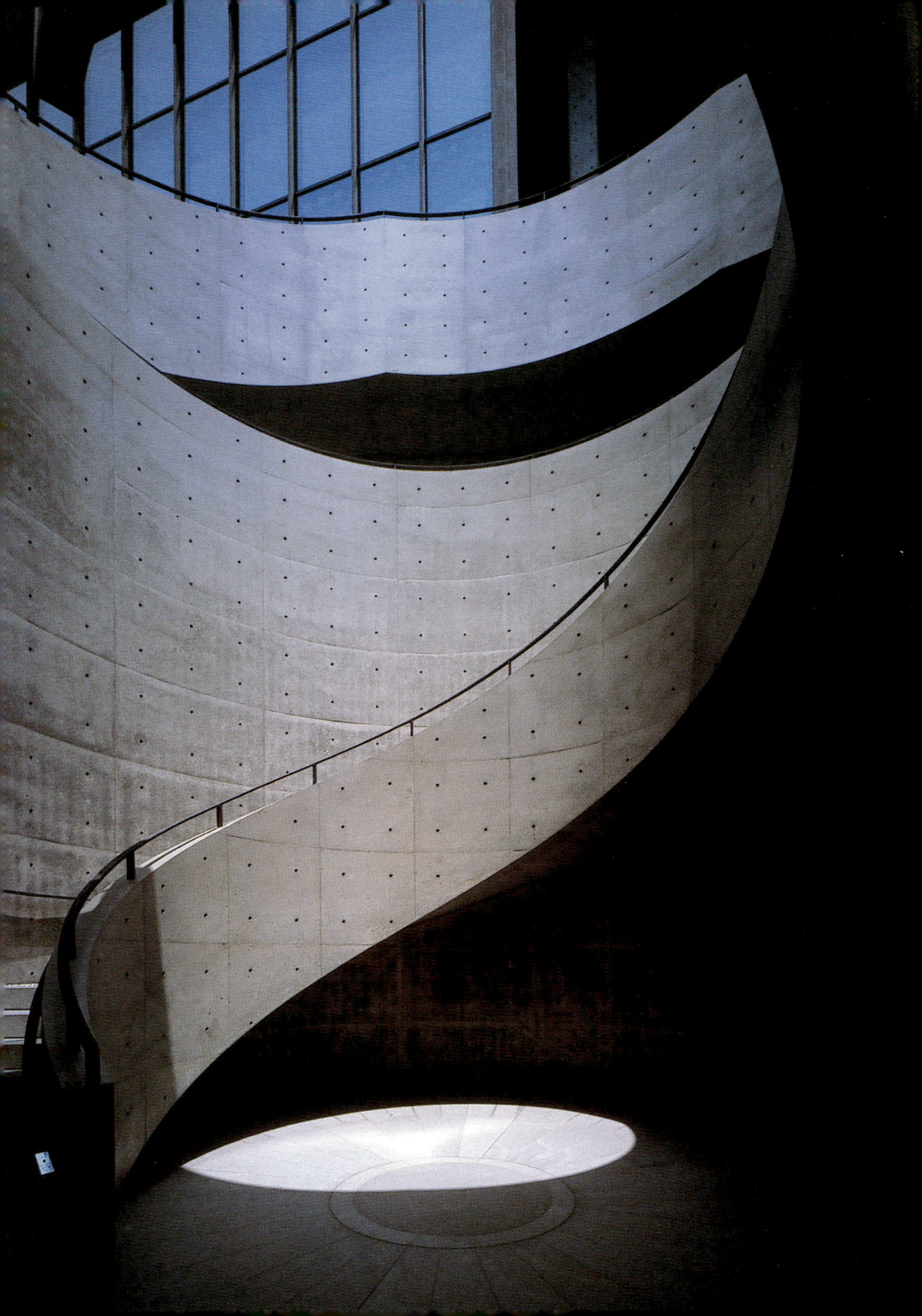

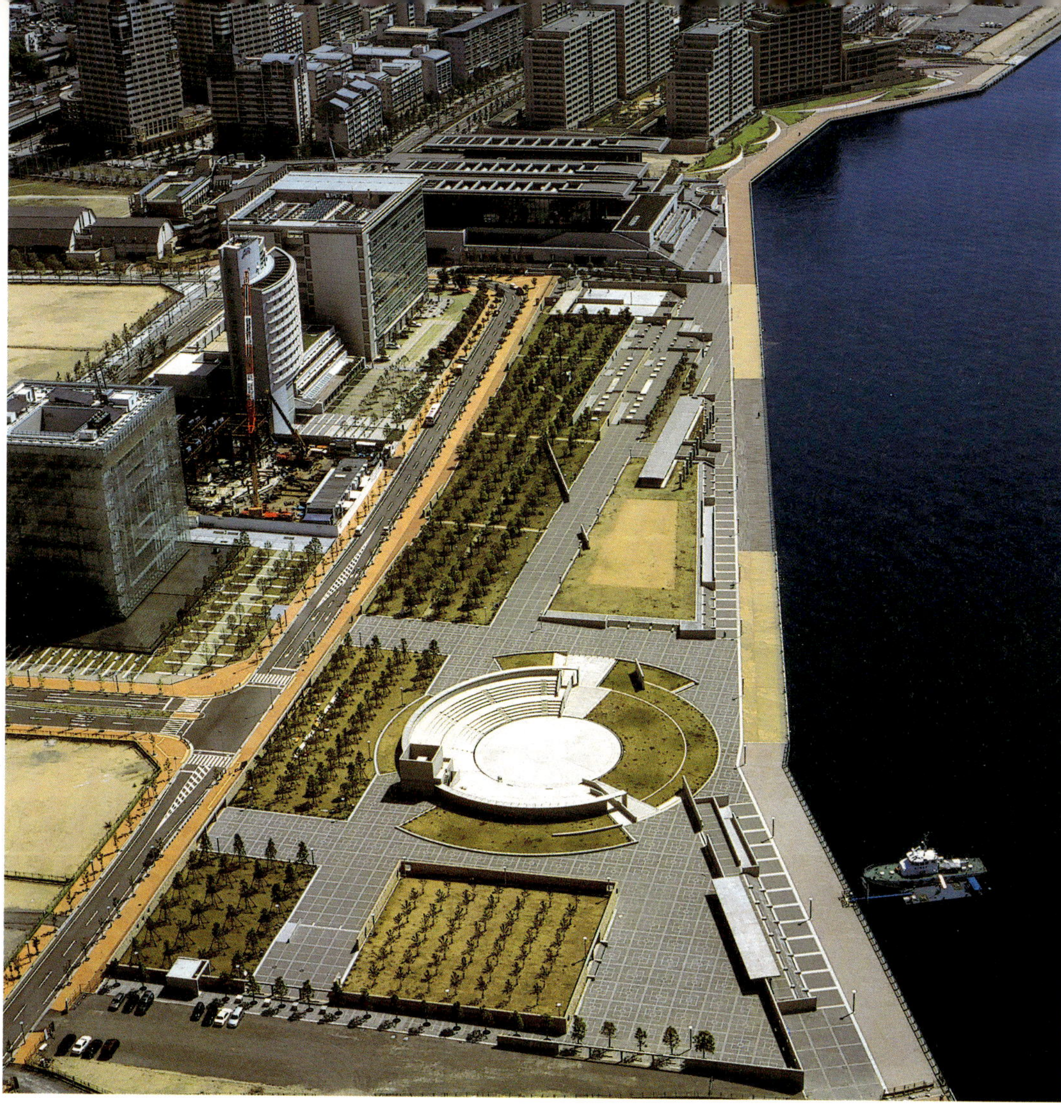

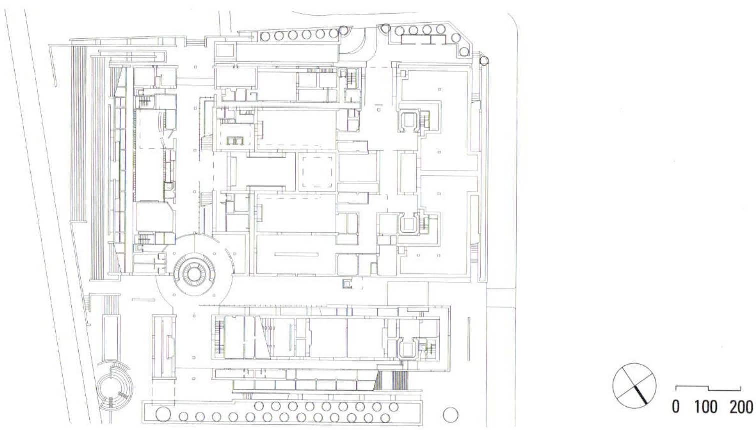

Ground floor
Erdgeschoss
Rez-de-chaussée
Piano terra

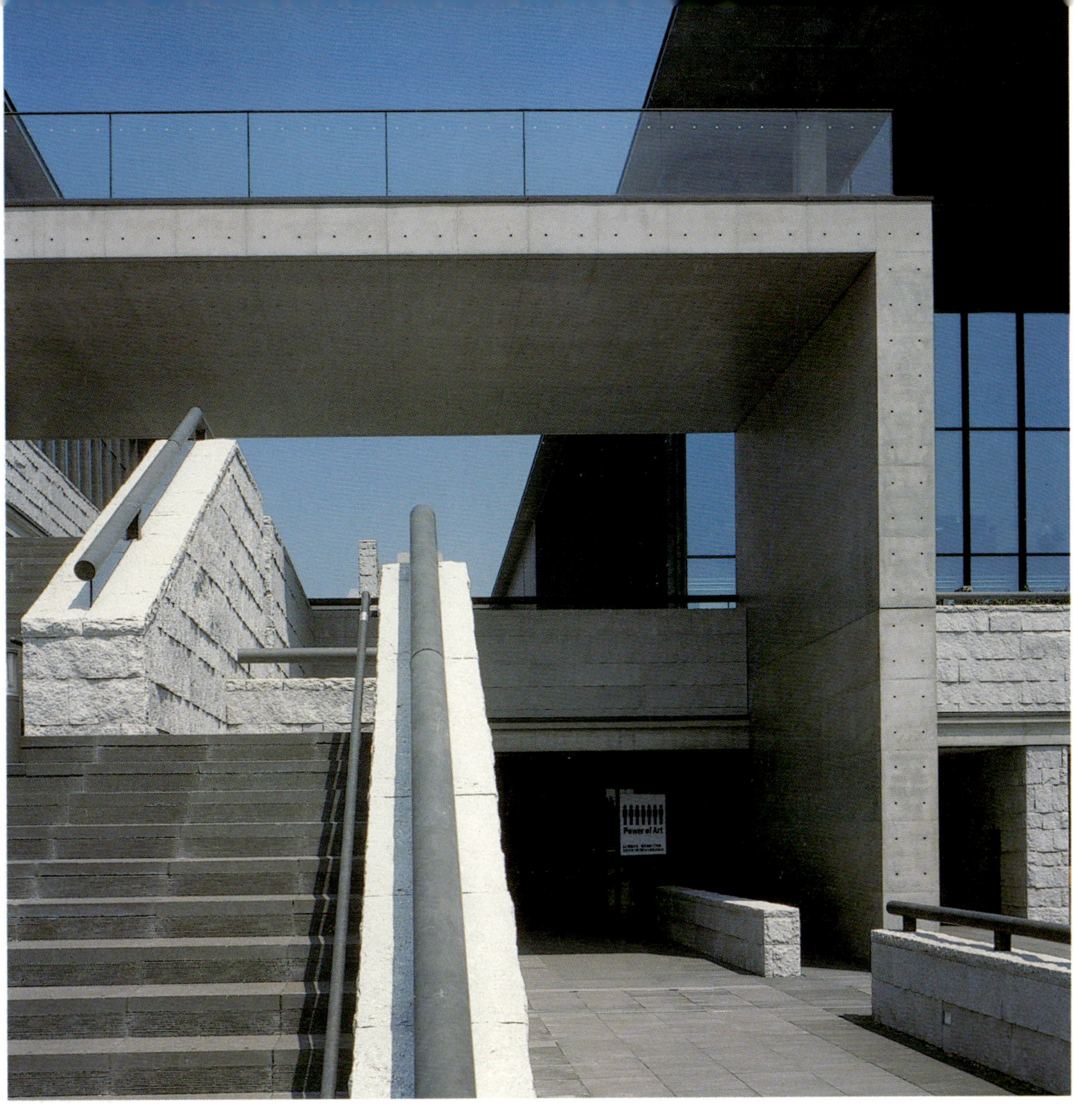

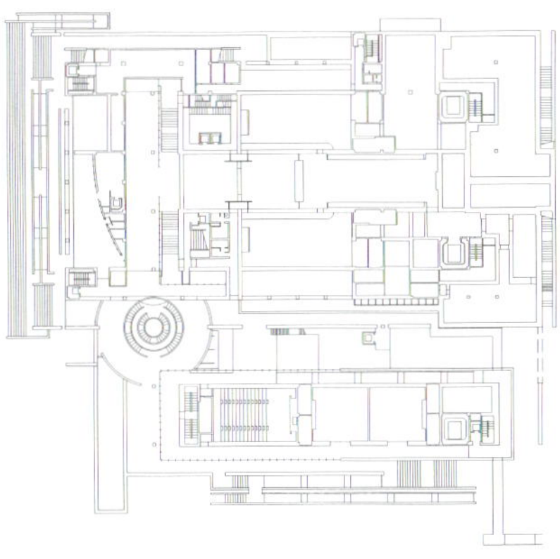

First floor
Erstes Obergeschoss
Premier étage
Piano primo

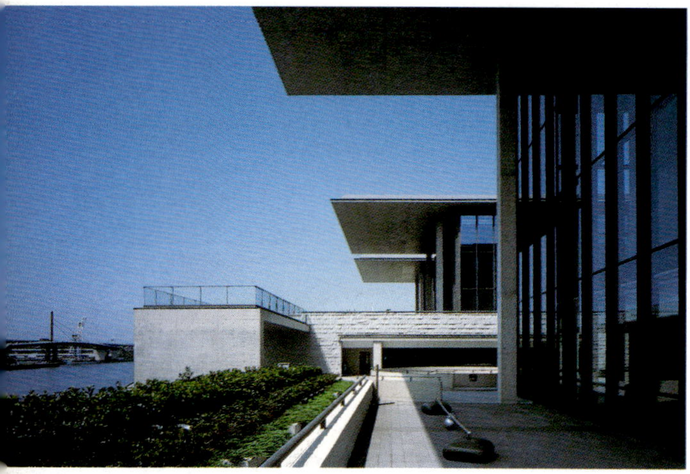

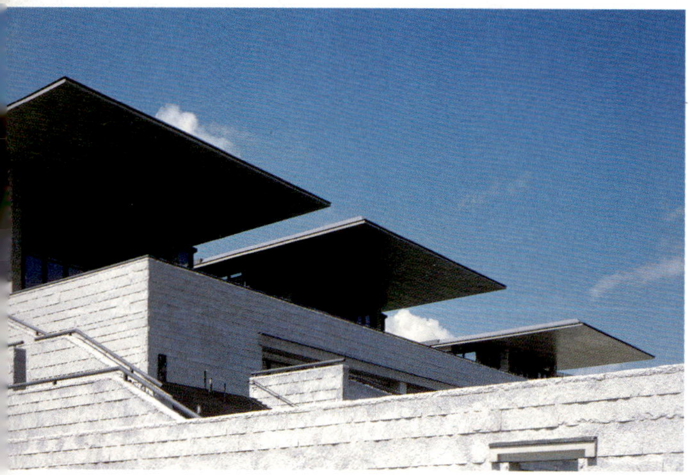

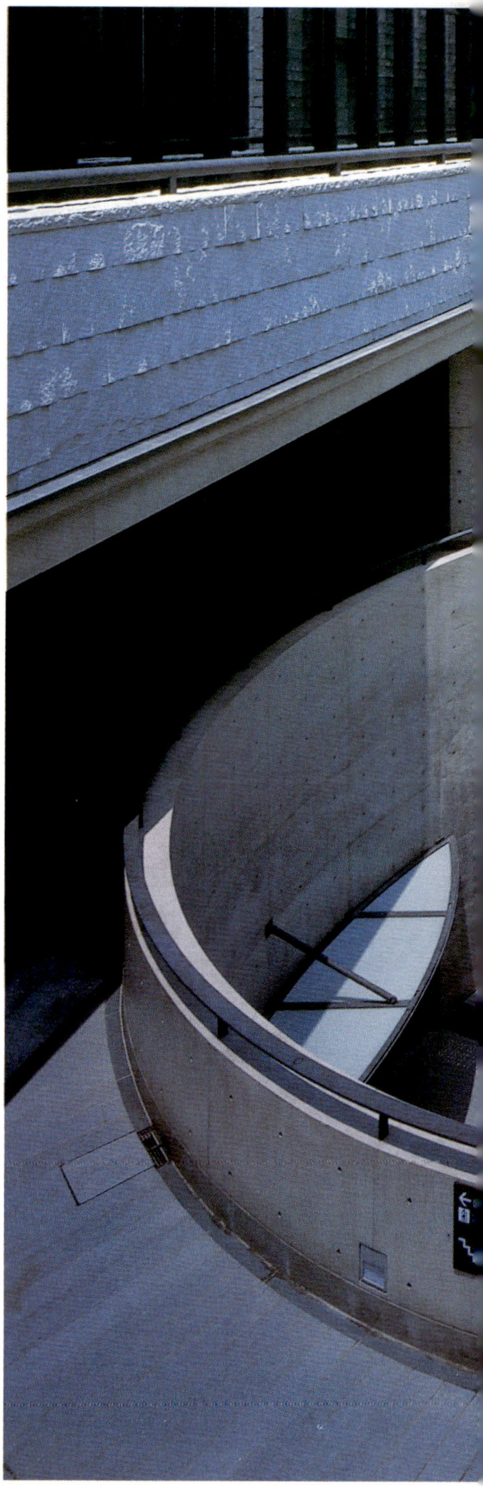

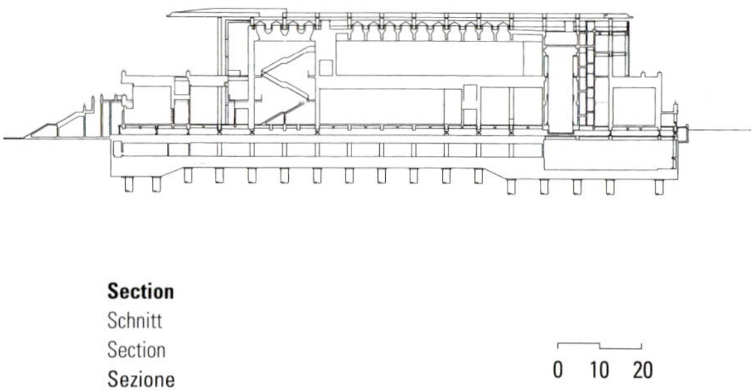

Section
Schnitt
Section
Sezione

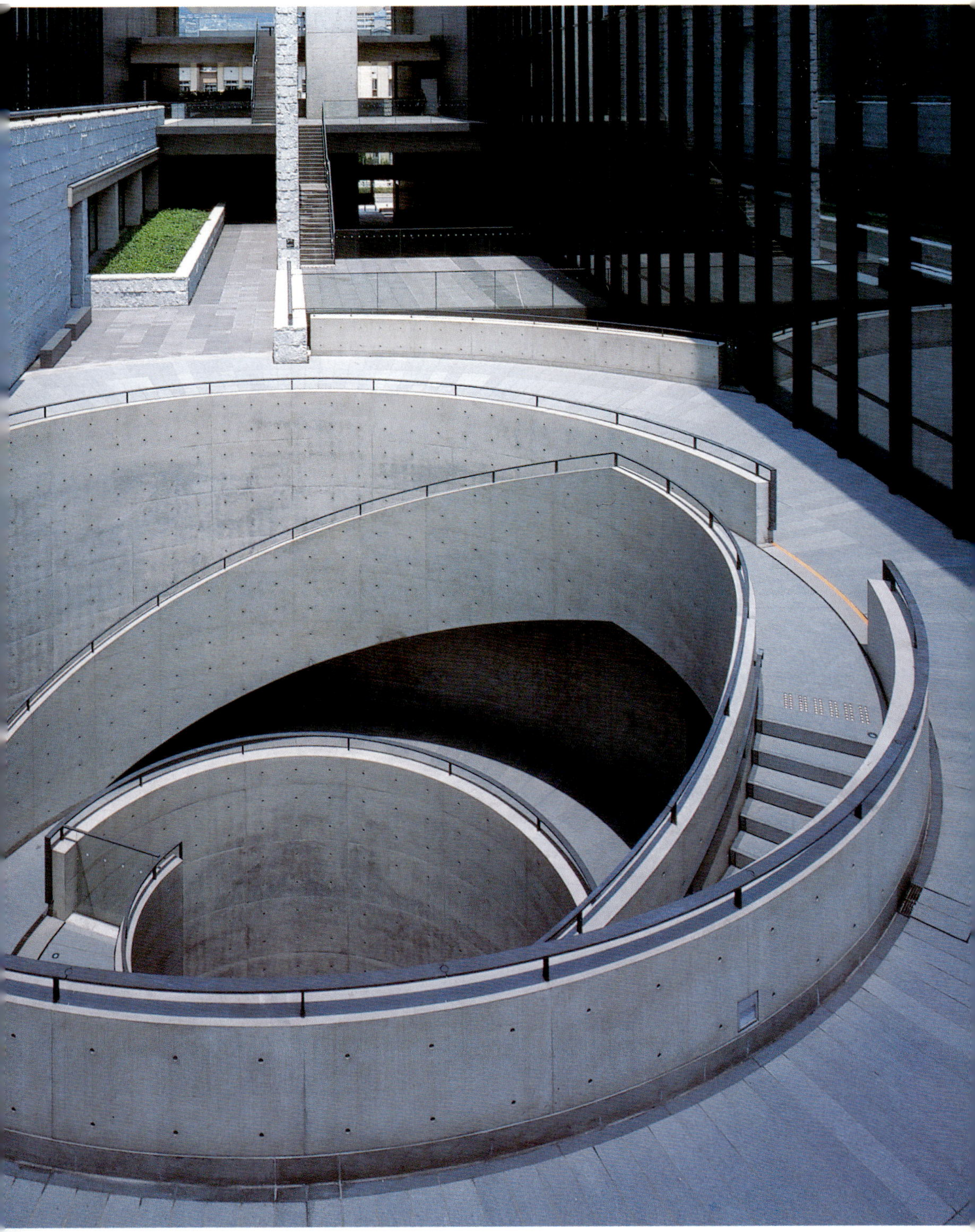

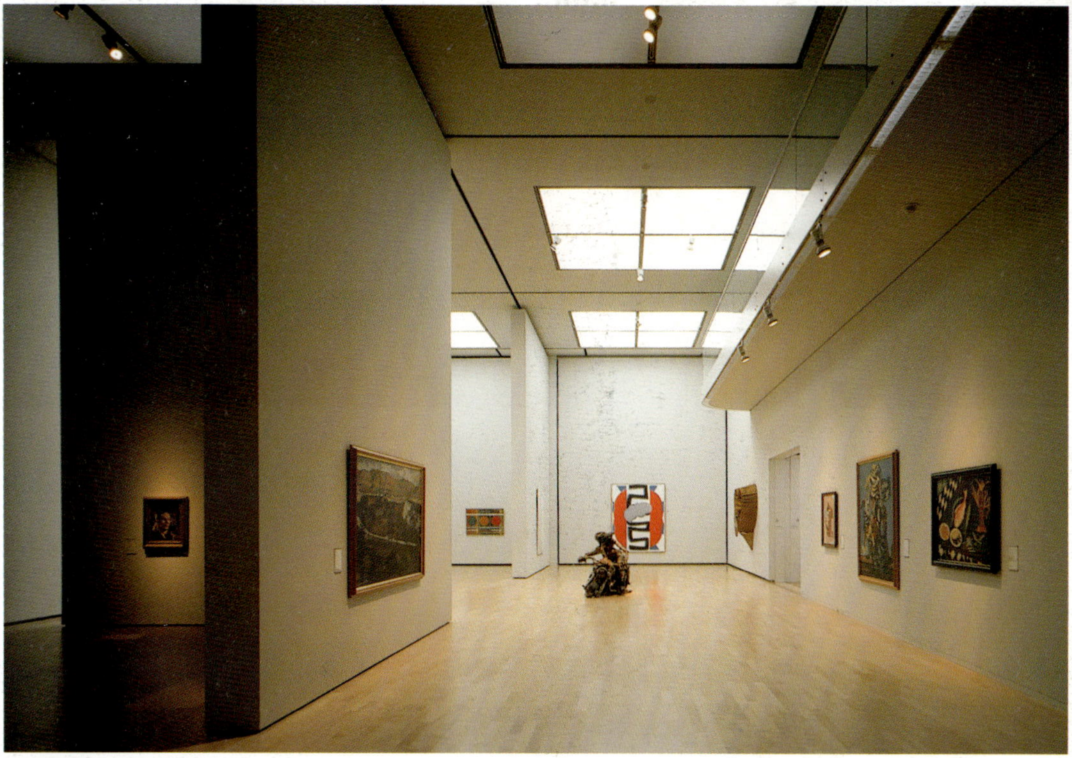

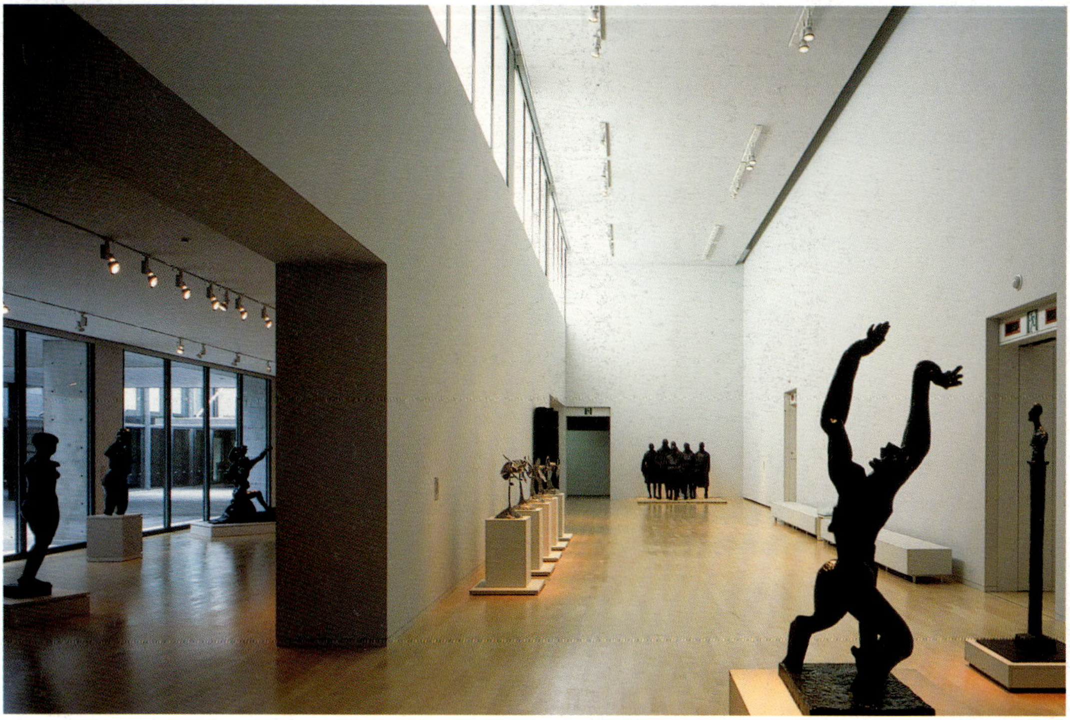

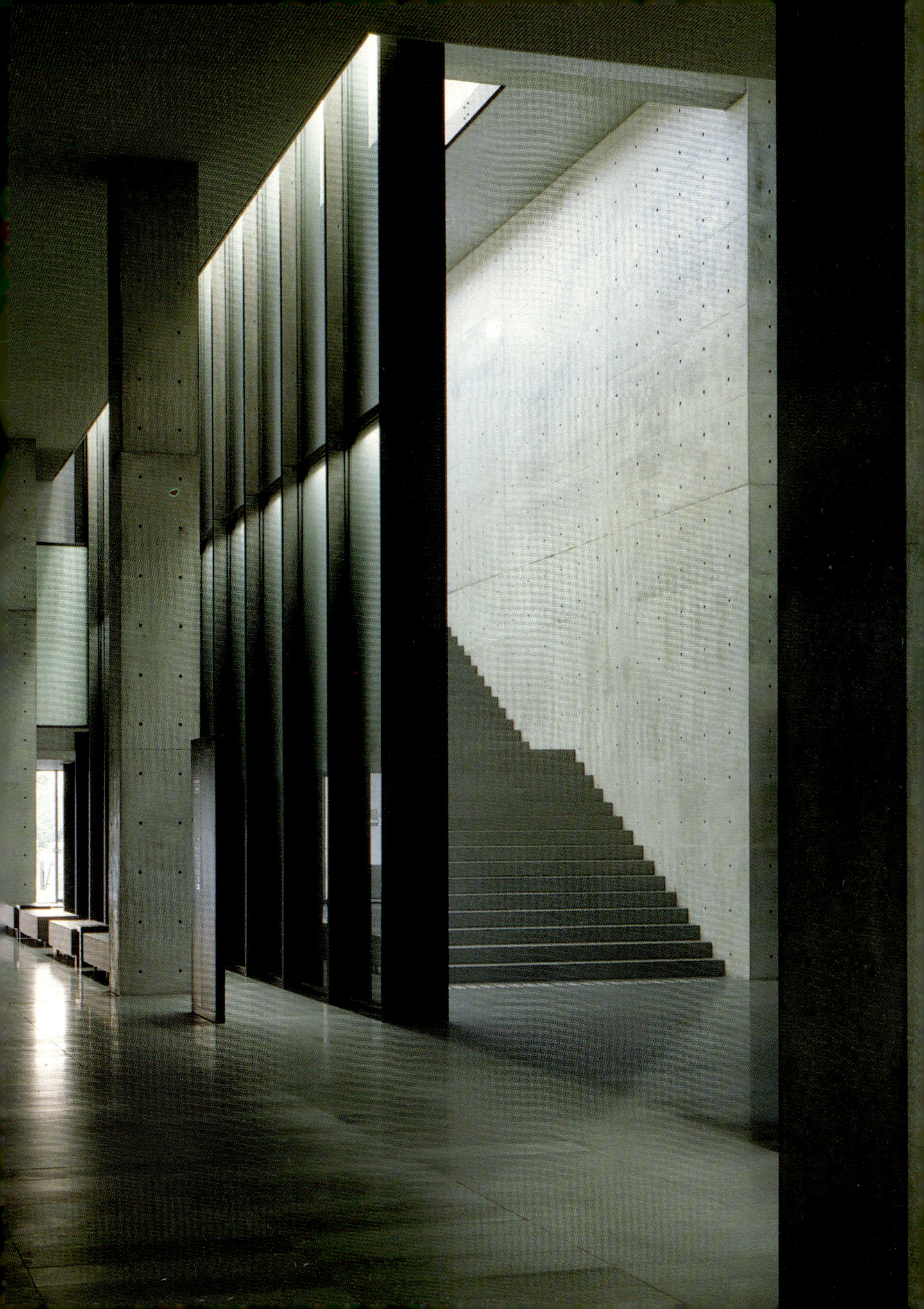

Modern Art Museum of Fort Worth

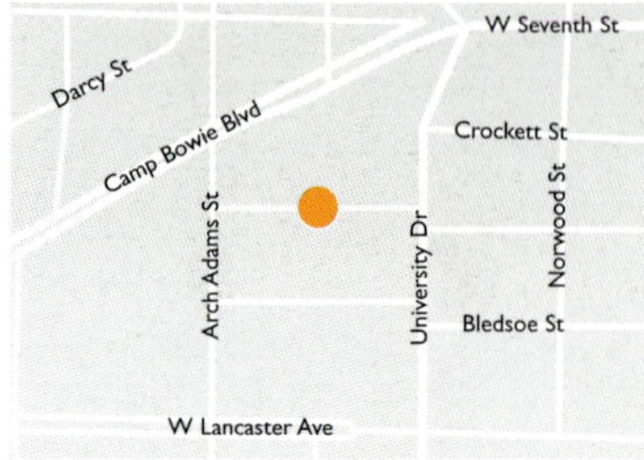

Location: Fort Worth, Texas, USA
Date of construction: 1999–2002
Photographer: Mitsuo Matsuoka

This project is located on the outskirts of Fort Worth, Texas, in the center of a large park, adjacent to one of the masterworks of the twentieth-century, the Kimbell Art Museum by Louis Kahn. Naturally, the major challenge of the design was to provide a harmonious relationship between itself and Kimbell's. The strategy Ando used was one of generating a project diluting any strict border between interior and exterior and—importantly—to make the rooms appropriate for the display of art objects. What was drawn up was a bucolic setting that contains a pond, a garden, and a wood that isolate the complex from the bustle of four-wheeled vehicles. The new museum comprises five rectangular concrete bays enclosed by glass façades. Two of these structures were to be used as public and administration areas, the remaining three as exhibition areas. The concrete, with its climatic and structural stability, contrasts with the glass, with its more fragile and intense relationship with the environment. Blending the two materials offers a great variety of settings, using many different types of transparencies and lightings.

Der Neubau sollte in den Außenbezirken von Fort Worth, Texas, mitten in einem großen Park errichtet werden, in unmittelbarer Nähe eines der Meisterwerke der Architektur des 20. Jahrhunderts, dem Kimbell Art Museum von Louis Kahn. Daher bestand die größte Herausforderung natürlich darin, ein ausgewogenes Verhältnis zwischen dem Neubau und dem Kimbell Art Museum zu erreichen. Ando entschied sich für ein Projekt, bei dem die Grenze zwischen innen und außen verschwimmt und alle Räume für die Ausstellung von Kunstwerken geeignet sind. Er entwarf eine bukolische Landschaft mit einem Teich, einem Garten und einem Wäldchen, das den Komplex vor dem Lärm des Autoverkehrs abschirmt. Drei der fünf rechteckigen Baukörper aus Beton mit Glasfassaden nehmen Ausstellungsräume auf, die beiden anderen öffentliche Einrichtungen und Büros. Der Beton als Baumaterial verleiht den Gebäuden Festigkeit und Klimabeständigkeit, während das Glas eine intensive Beziehung zur Außenwelt erlaubt. Aus der Kombination beider Materialien erwächst eine große Bandbreite von Stimmungen, Durchblicken und Lichteffekten.

Le site de ce projet se trouve dans la banlieue de Fort Worth, Texas, au cœur d'un grand parc et juste à côté d'une des œuvres maîtresses de l'architecture du XXème siècle : le Musée d'art Kimbell de Louis Kahn. Naturellement, le principal défi conceptuel était de créer une bonne relation entre le nouvel édifice et le Kimbell. La stratégie a porté sur la génération d'un projet où la frontière intérieur–extérieur serait diluée et pour lequel tous les espaces seraient aptes à l'exposition d'œuvres d'art. Un environnement bucolique a été conçu, incluant un étang, un jardin et un bois, isolant l'ensemble des nuisances de la circulation environnante. Dans ce cadre, cinq volumes rectangulaires ont été construits avec une structure en béton enveloppée de façades vitrées. Deux d'entre eux ont été destinés à l'administration et à des affectations publiques, ainsi l'auditoire et le café. Les trois autres accueillent les espaces d'expositions. Le béton apporte une certaine stabilité climatique et structurelle au projet, alors que le verre entretient une intense relation avec l'environnement. Leur combinaison offre tout un éventail d'atmosphères aux transparences et éclairages divers.

Il terreno di questo edificio si trova alla periferia di Fort Worth, Texas, in mezzo a un grande parco, proprio accanto ad uno dei capolavori dell'architettura del XX° secolo: il Museo d'Arte Kimbell di Louis Kahn. Naturalmente la sfida principale della progettazione era stabilire una relazione armoniosa tra il nuovo edificio ed il Kimbell. La strategia è stata quella di creare un progetto dove la frontiera tra interno ed esterno si dissolvesse e dove tutti gli spazi fossero adatti all'esposizione di opere d'arte. É stato progettato uno spazio naturale che comprende uno stagno d'acqua, un giardino ed un bosco che isolano il complesso dal rumoroso traffico veicolare. Inoltre sono stati eretti cinque volumi rettangolari con struttura di cemento e vetrate; due di loro sono stati destinati ad attività amministrative e ai servizi per il publico ed i rimanenti tre, a sale d'esposizione. Il cemento con la sua stabilità climatica e strutturale contrasta con il vetro e la sua più fragile ed intensa relazione con l'ambiente. La combinazione di entrambi offre una gran varietà di ambienti, con differenti trasparenze e luci.

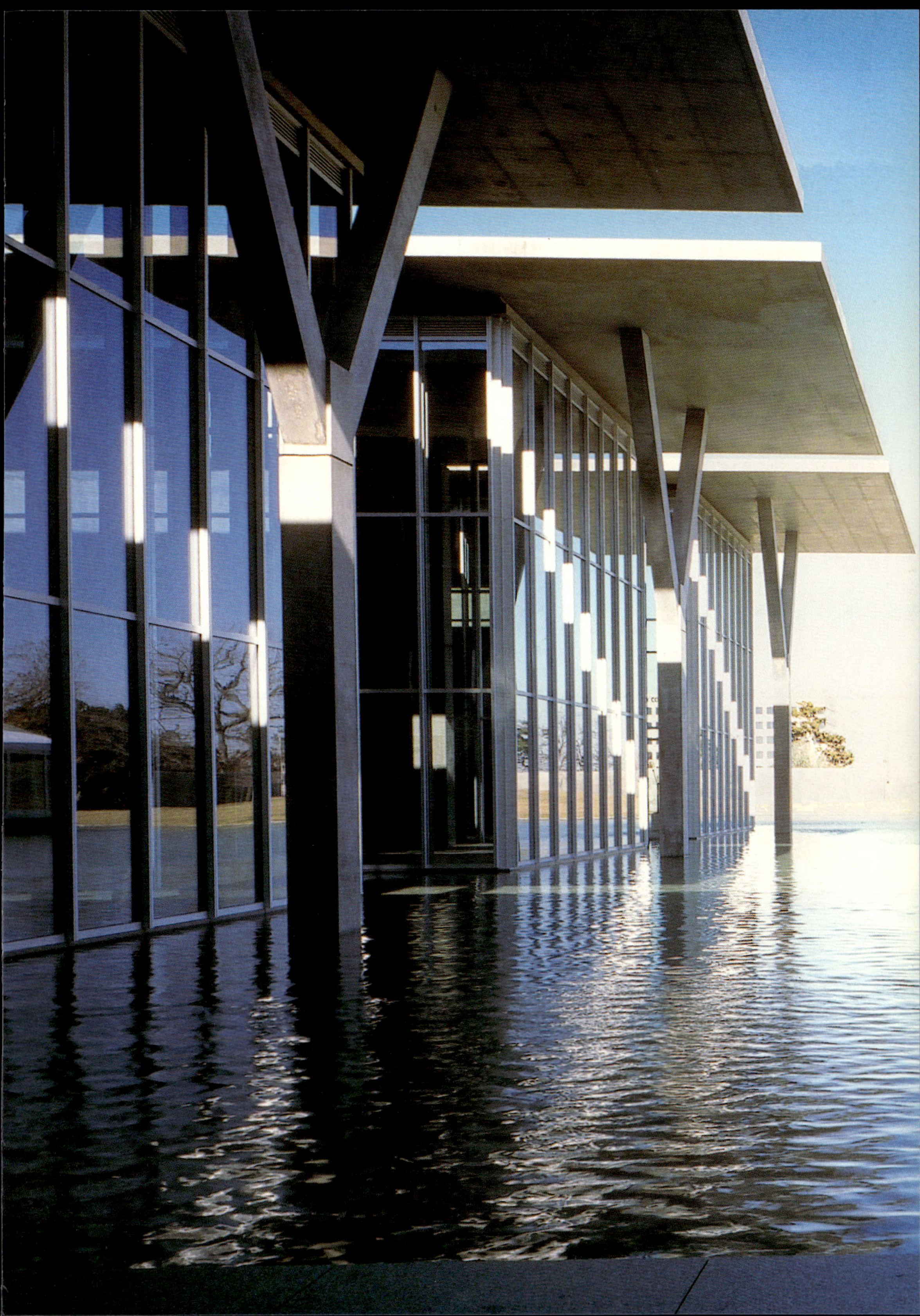

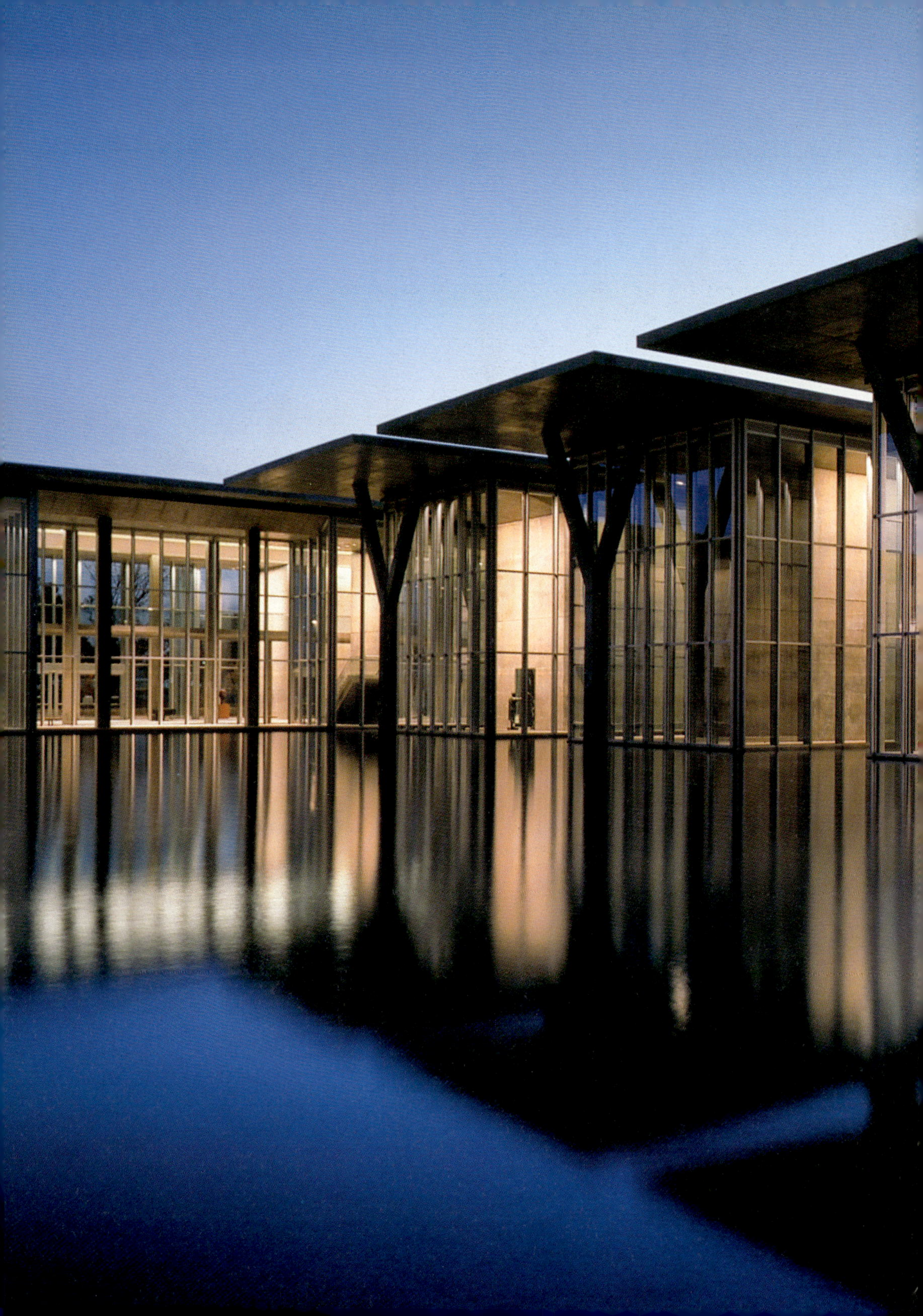

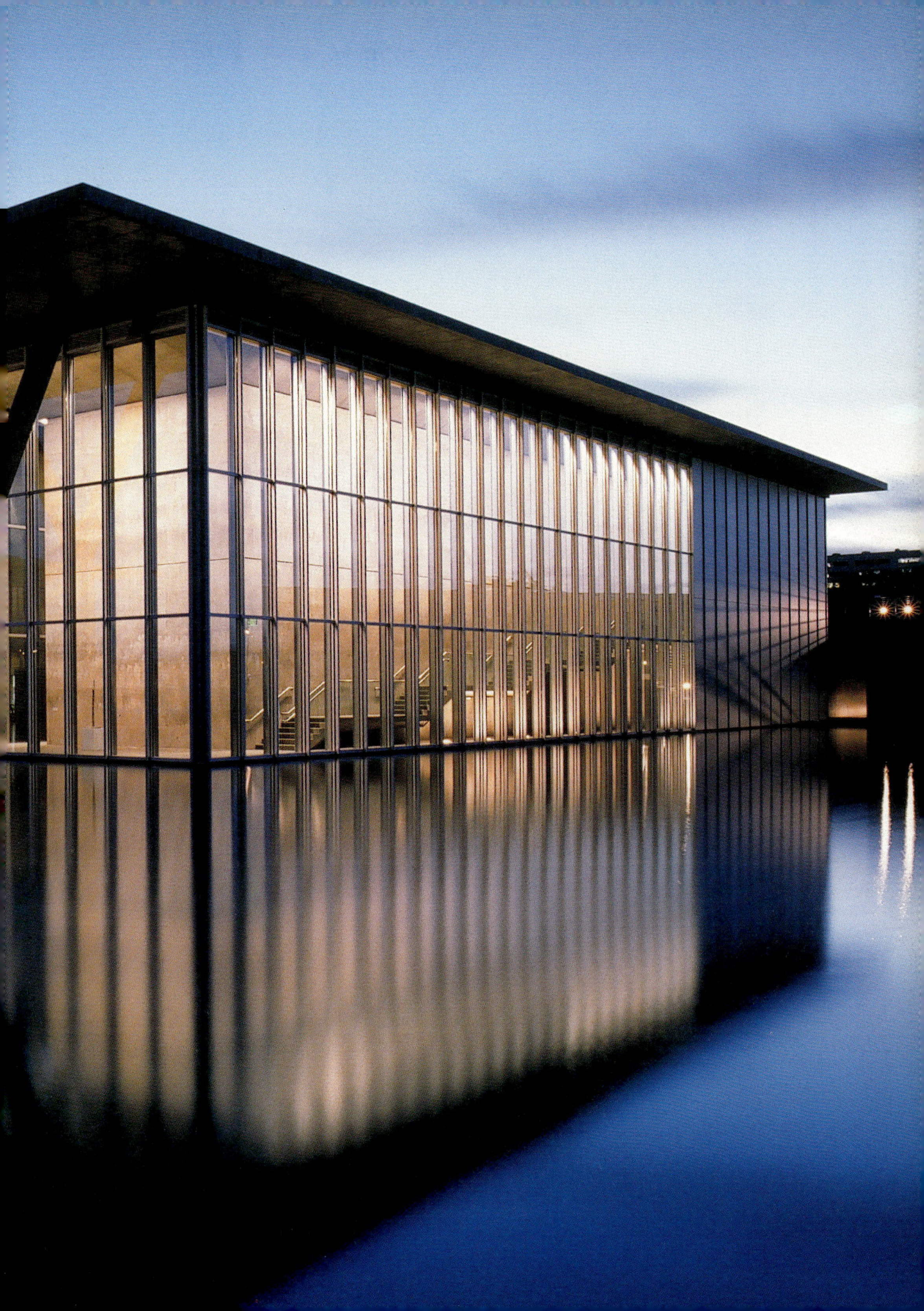

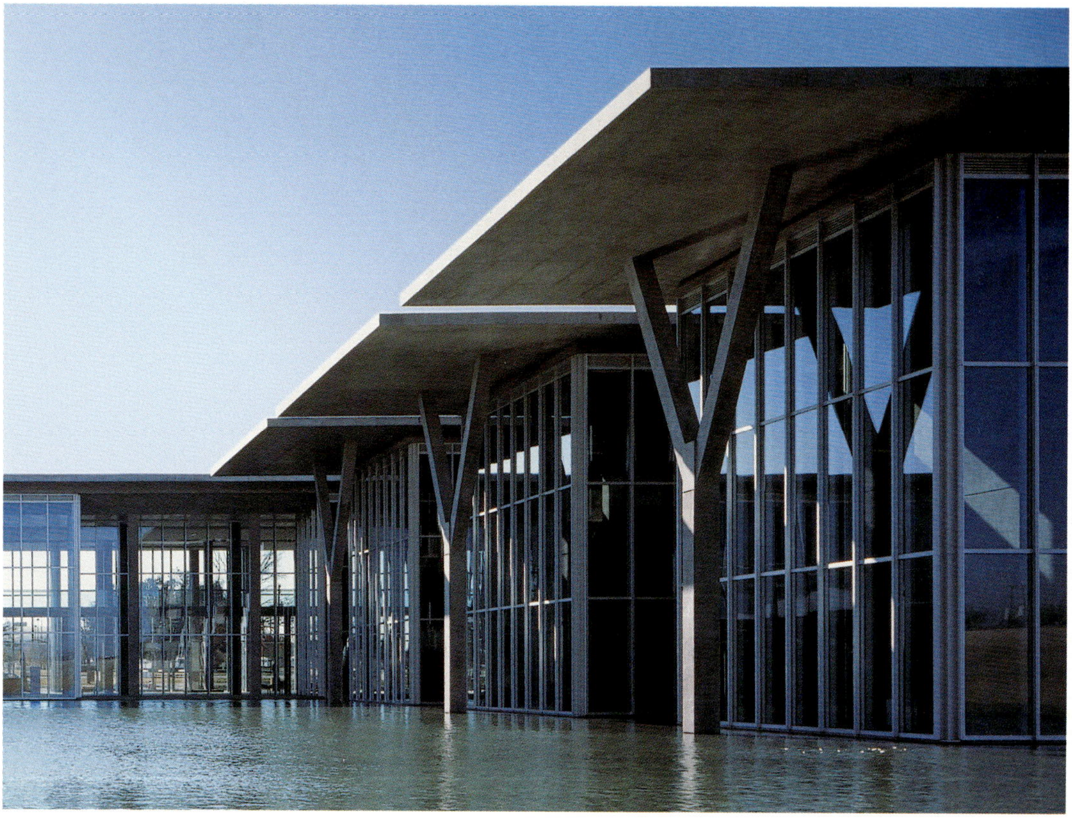

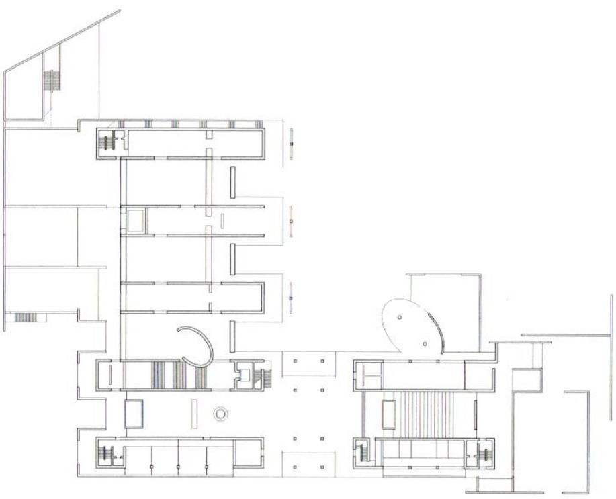

Ground floor
Rez-de-chaussée
Erdgeschoss
Piano terra

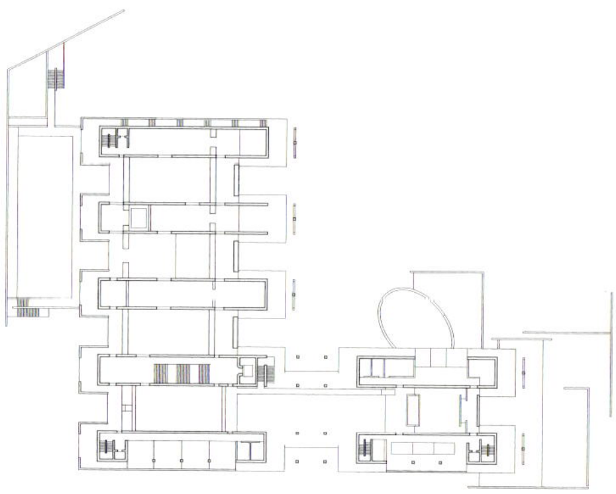

First floor
Erstes Obergeschoss
Premier étage
Piano primo

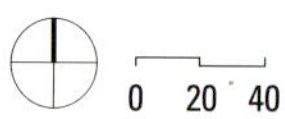

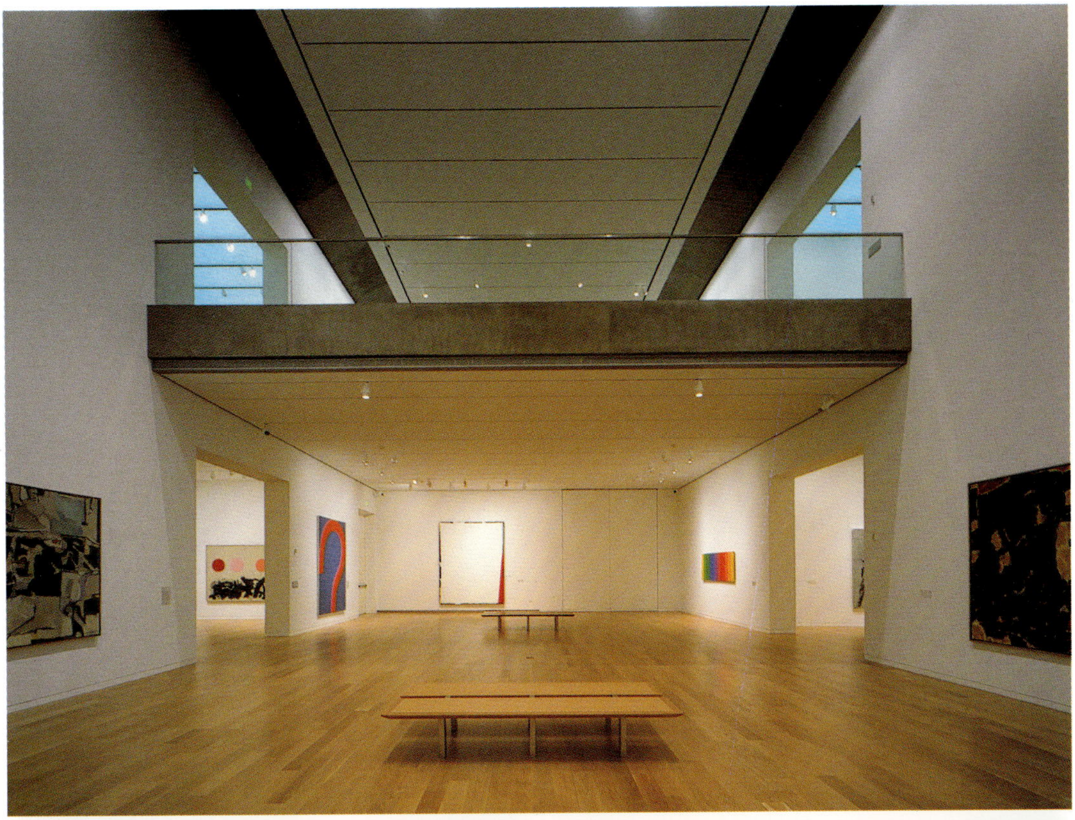

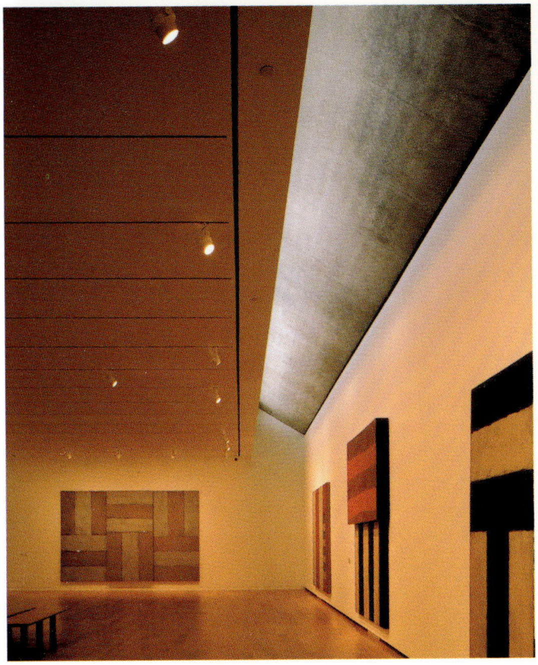

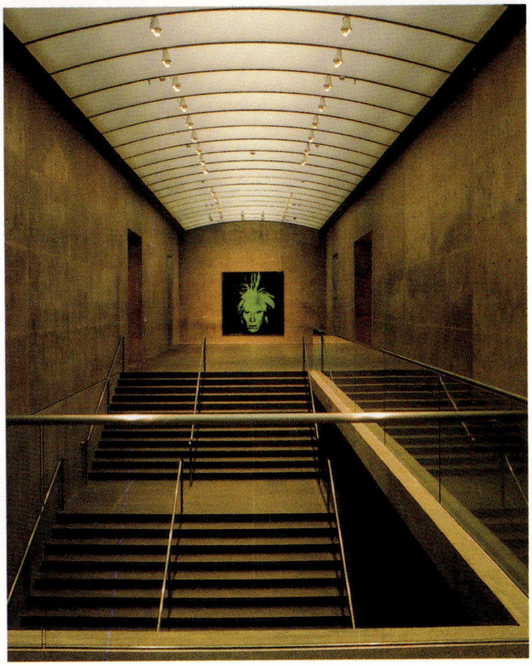

Shiba Ryotaro Memorial Museum

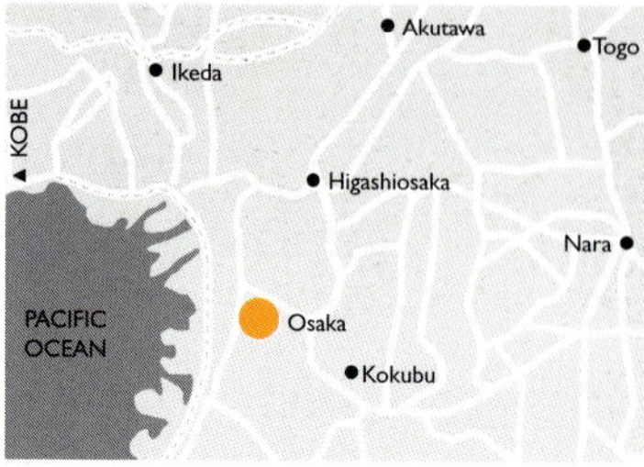

Location: Higashiosaka, Japan
Date of construction: 2000–2001
Photographer: Shigeo Ogawa

Ryotaro Shiba is one of post-war Japan's most important literary figures. His works played a decisive role in renewing the spirits of the population during such a dramatic time. The museum erected in his honor is an institution whose role is one of passing his legacy on to future generations. The site chosen for the project is next to the writer's house, in a residential area surrounded by well-tended woods. What the design seeks to do is to create a space that will materialize Shiba's theories and simultaneously provide a home for the extensive collection of books he amassed. The hall is a curved piece half of which is below grade and accessed by a glassed corridor from which the lushness of the surrounding vegetation is visible. Inside the building the trajectory, which is accompanied by a drop in the level of the lighting, ends in a large triple-height space occupied only by the writer's shelved books. The only opening in this large library is comprised of a stained-glass window generating a rich and varied play of light. It is a fitting symbol of the diversity and wealth of Ryotaro Shiba's thought.

Ryotaro Shiba war einer der bedeutendsten Literaten im Japan der Nachkriegszeit. Seine Werke spielten eine entscheidende Rolle, als es darum ging, dem Volk in der schwierigen Zeit damals wieder neuen Mut zu geben. Das ihm zu Ehren errichtete Museum soll zukünftigen Generationen sein Erbe nahebringen. Es wurde neben dem Haus des Schriftstellers in einem Wohnviertel mit altem Baumbestand erbaut. Beim Entwurf ging es darum, einen Raum zu schaffen, der Shibas Theorien versinnbildlichen und zugleich seine umfangreiche Büchersammlung aufnehmen sollte. Der geschwungene, halb im Boden versenkte Bau ist über einen gläsernen Korridor zugänglich, der durch die üppige Vegetation des Gartens führt. Am Ende dieses Ganges nimmt das Licht im inneren des Gebäudes ab und man gelangt in einen über drei Geschosse reichenden Raum, dessen Wände völlig mit Bücherregalen bedeckt sind. Die einzige Öffnung des Bibliotheksraums besteht in den aus Scheiben unterschiedlicher Form und Größe zusammengesetzten Glasfenstern, die ein vielfältiges Licht- und Schattenspiel erzeugen und somit ein Symbol sind für die Mannigfaltigkeit der reichen Gedankenwelt Ryotaro Shibas.

Ryotaro Shiba fût l'un des écrivains les plus importantes du Japon de l'après-guerre. Ses œuvres ont joué un rôle décisif de motivation de la population durant cette période si dramatique. Le musée érigé en son honneur est une institution dont la finalité est la transmission de son legs aux générations futures. Le site choisi pour le projet se trouve juste à côté de la maison de l'écrivain, dans un quartier résidentiel entourée de merveilleux bosquets. La conception avait pour objet de créer un espace à même de matérialiser les théories de Shiba tout en accueillant la vaste collection d'oeuvres qu'il avait lui-même constituée. L'édifice consiste en un volume incurvé semi enterré accessible par un couloir vitré, permettant de contempler la luxuriance de la végétation environnante. Le parcours, accompagné d'une diminution de la lumière, se termine dans un grand espace de triple hauteur, complètement occupé par les étagères de livres. La seule ouverture de cette grande bibliothèque est composée d'un vitrail, générant un spectre lumineux varié, symbole de la diversité et de la richesse de la pensée de Ryotaro Shiba.

Ryotaro Shiba è una delle figure letterarie più importanti del Giappone del dopoguerra. Le sue opere hanno svolto un ruolo decisivo nel rinvigorire l'animo della popolazione in un momento così drammatico. Il museo, eretto in suo onore, è un'istituzione, ed ha lo scopo di trasmettere la sua eredità alle generazioni future. Il terreno scelto per la costruzione è ubicato vicino alla casa dello scrittore, in una zona residenziale circondata da splendidi boschi. L'obiettivo del progetto era creare uno spazio che materializzasse le teorie di Shiba e che, allo stesso tempo, accogliesse l'ampia collezione di libri da lui posseduti. La costruzione è composta da un volume curvo seminterrato, al quale si accede attraverso un corridoio vetrato e dal quale si scorge la vegetazione circostante. Il tragitto, che si accompagna ad una diminuzione della luce, si conclude in un grande spazio a triplice altezza completamente occupato da scaffalature piene di libri. L'unica apertura di questa grande biblioteca è costituita da una vetrata che genera un assortito spettro di luci, simbolo della diversità e ricchezza del pensiero di Ryotaro Shiba.

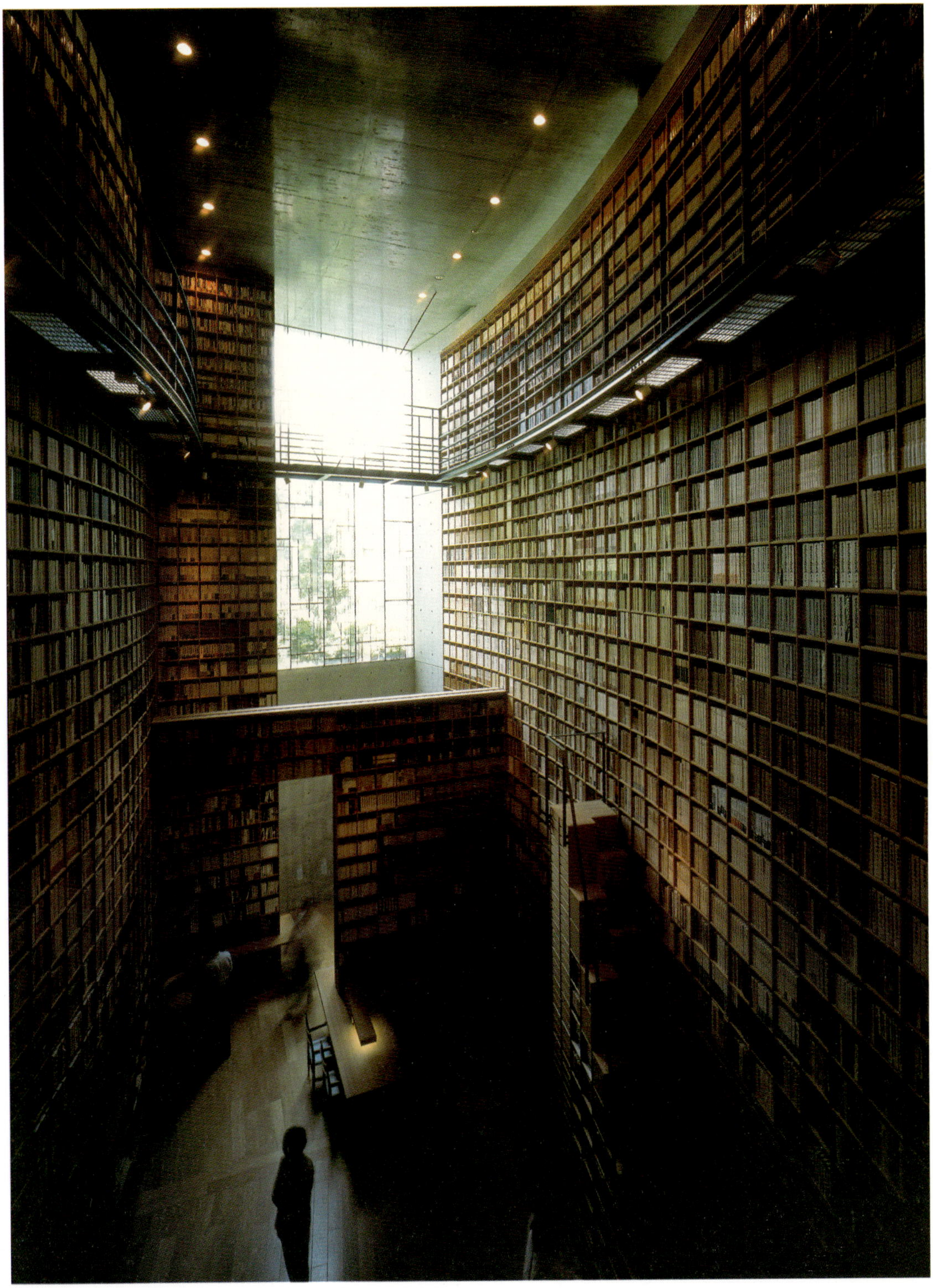

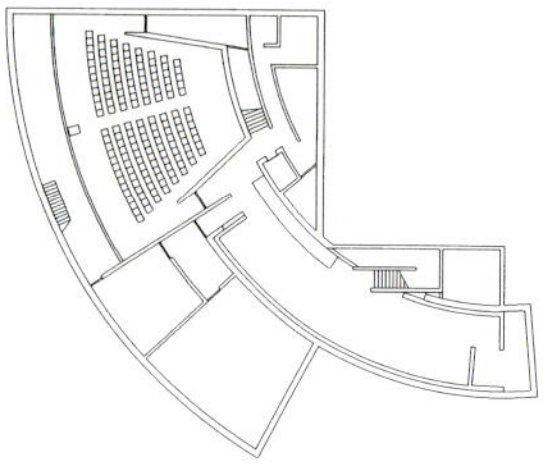

Basement Souterrain
Sous-sol **Piano interrato**

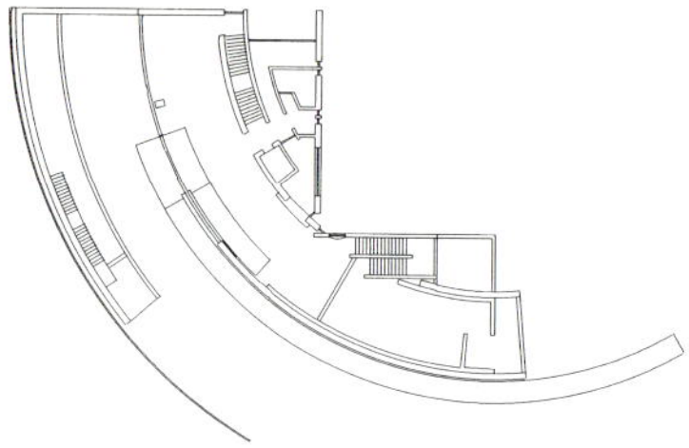

Ground floor Erdgeschoss
Rez-de-chaussée **Piano terra**

0 5 10

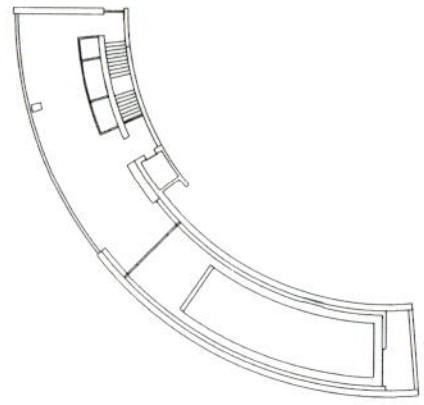

First floor Erstes Obergeschoss
Premier étage **Piano primo**

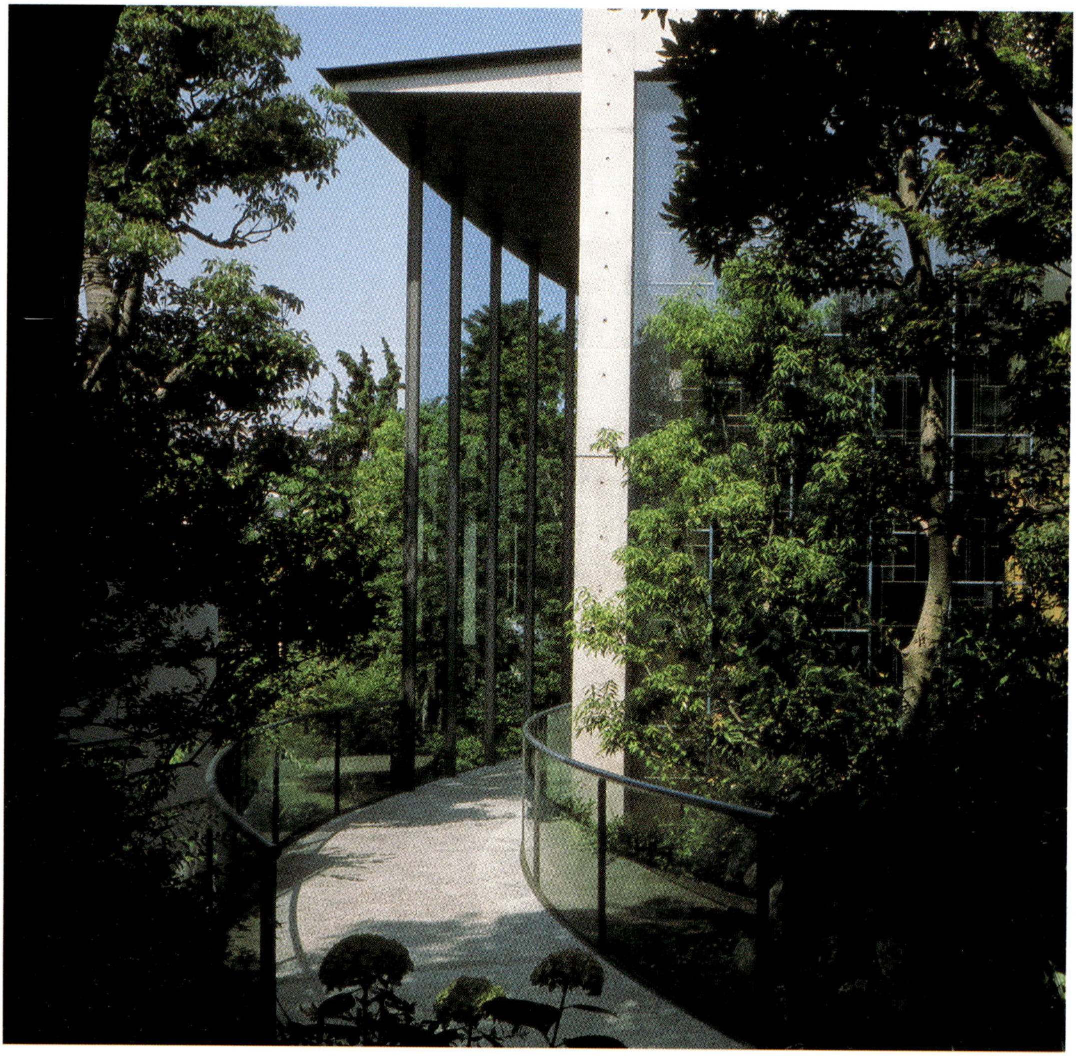

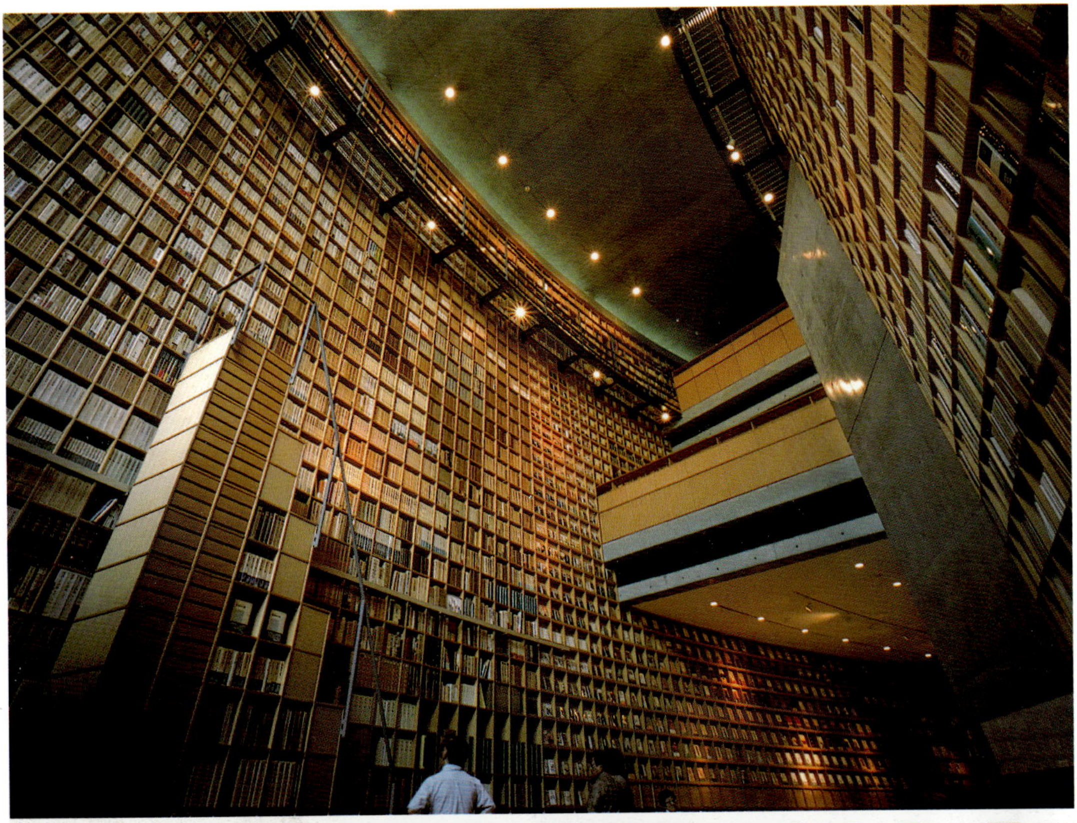

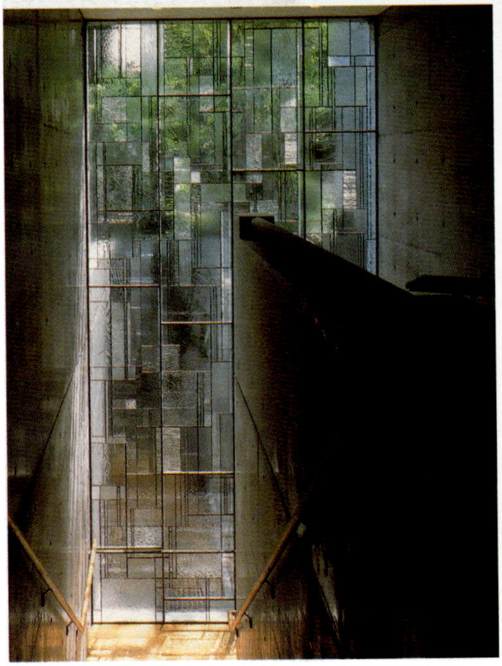

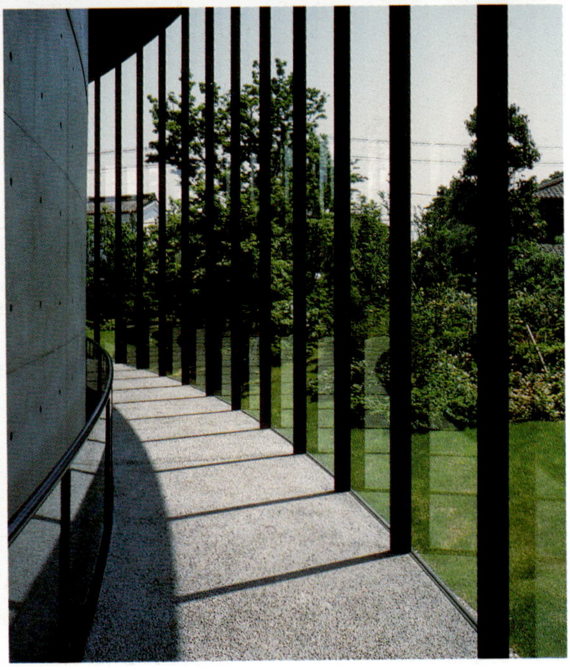

Hombroich Museum

Location: Neuss, Nordrheim-Westfalen, Germany
Date of construction: 2002–2004
Photographer: Tadao Ando

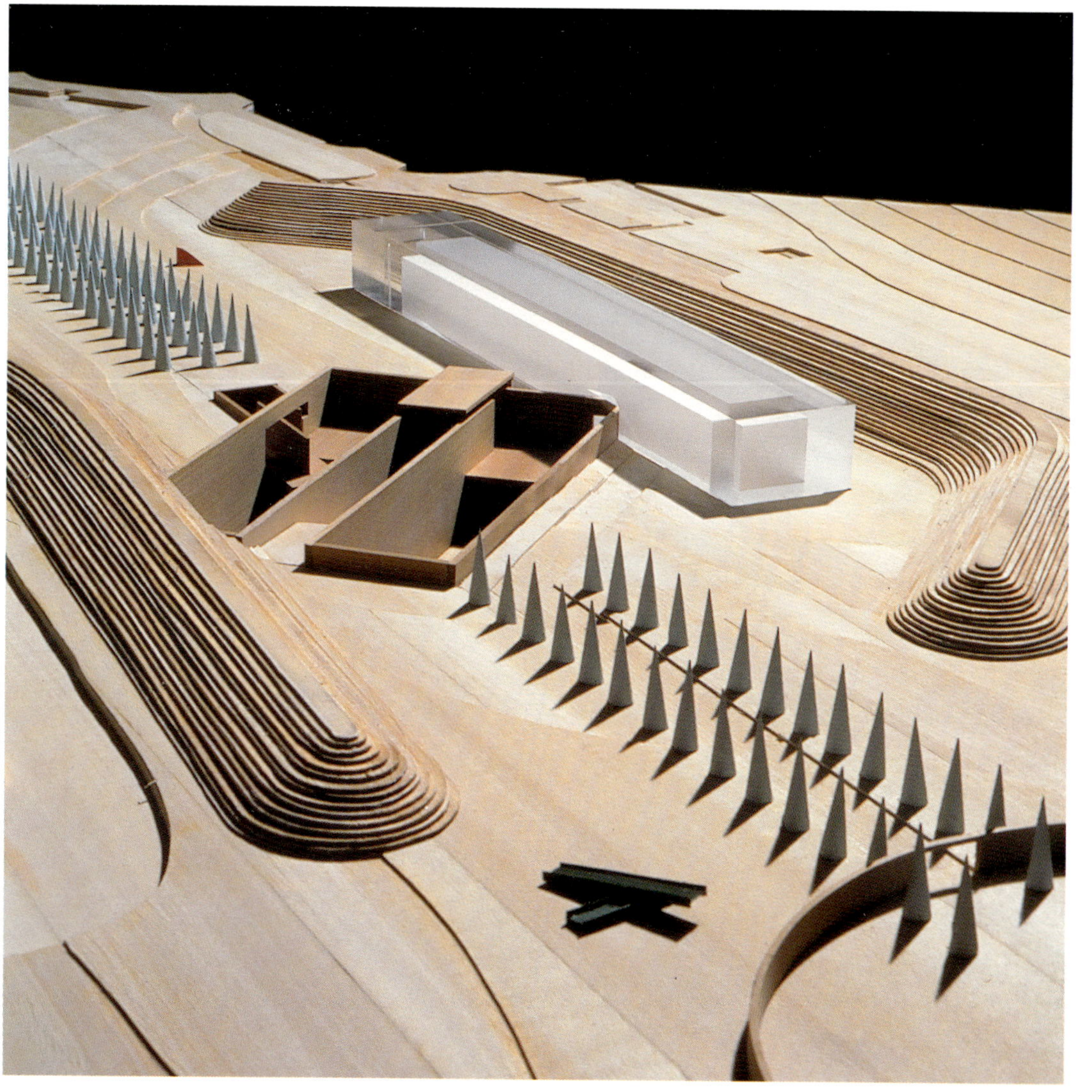

Fondation François Pinault pour l'Art Contemporain

Location: Seguin, Hauts-de-Seine, France
Date of construction: 2004–2006
Photographer: Tomio Ohashi

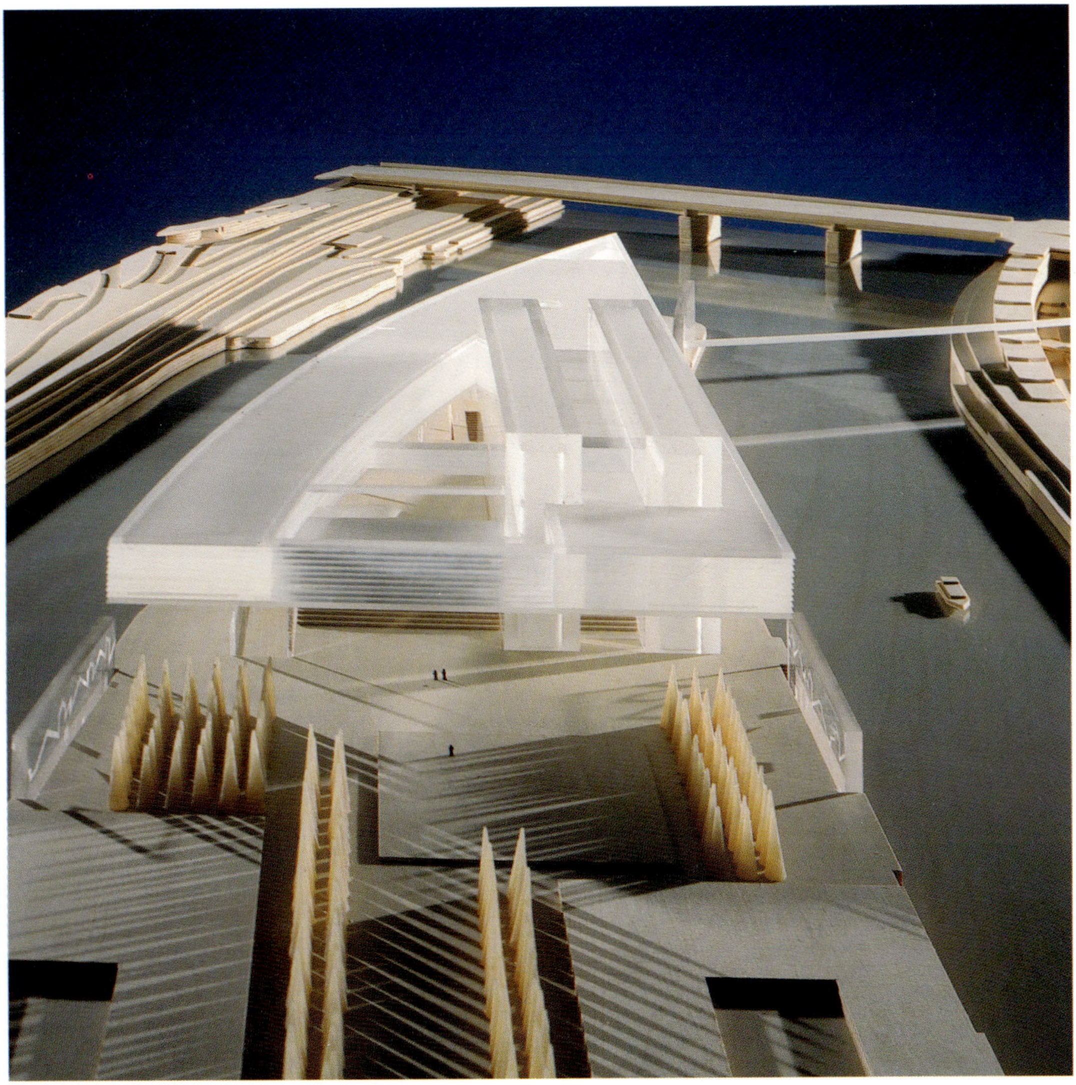